BITTERS

Rebecca Seiferle

COPPER
CANYON
PRESS

Printed in the United States of America.

Cover art: *Aconitum*. Copyright 2001 Karl Blossfeldt Archiv-Ann ünd Jürgen Wilde, Zülpich, Köln/ARS New York

Copper Canyon Press is in residence under the auspices of the Centrum Foundation at Fort Worden State Park in Port Townsend, Washington. Centrum sponsors artist residencies, education workshops for Washington State students and teachers, blues, jazz, and fiddle tunes festivals, classical music performances, and The Port Townsend Writers' Conference.

LIBRARY OF CONGRESS CATALOGING-IN-PUBLICATION DATA

Seiferle, Rebecca.
Bitters / Rebecca Seiferle.
  p. cm.
ISBN 1-55659-168-3
1. Title.
PS3569.E533 B5 2001
811'.54 – DC21

                                        2001004489

9 8 7 6 5 4 3 2 FIRST PRINTING

COPPER CANYON PRESS
Post Office Box 271
Port Townsend, Washington 98368
www.coppercanyonpress.org

Contents

MY MOTHER'S HIP

THE SACRIFICE TREE

POÈTE MAUDIT

THE GIFT

Bitters

Proviso

Pyrus Malus—an evil fire?—burning
in the branches, perhaps, of a primitive
species of crab-apple, cultivated
in all temperate zones into so many
varieties: the apple of discord
awarded to the fairest (in beauty
not justice) who caused the burning of Troy,
the apple of Sodom that Josephus
claimed dissolved into smoke and ashes
when grasped by a traveler's hand,
Adam's apple, the *apple of love*,
the *apple of the eye*, the *Apple John*
said to be perfect only when shriveled,
any number of erroneous fruits, any
disappointing thing. *"Faith (as you say)*
there's small choice in rotten apples" or
"Feed an enemy the skin of a peach,
a friend the skin of an apple." But tree
of knowledge or morning snack, you can have
the gala skin, the blush of the apple,
even the white succulent flesh, if you save
me the core—that earthly constellation
usually tossed to horses or thrown away.
I'll be with the Gypsies who cut to the star
of seeds at the heart of each orb, for
it's the core I want—intensely *apple*,
medicinal with a dash of arsenic, the zing
of earth, the crisp bite of becoming.

FACE

OF THE

LEVIATHAN

Seraphim

Even houseflies must have their angels.
Principalities, at knee or elbow, the voice
of God caught within an ear, at such a pitch,
it makes the skull hum. And if I swat them,
can they blame me? Like all good messengers,
they're just testing whether we are still alive.
By such means, the priest taught me, *God creates —*
all the living and the dead, just a nursery
for his hatching. So when I found a trinity
of maggots in the abdominal wall
of a living kitten, though I had to pinch
them out, I could not blame them — Shadrach,
Meshach, Abednego, pale witnesses
of a homesick God, caught in the furnace
of the flesh, hoping to sprout wings.

Comparative Religion

So many of the truly horrible accounts in the Bible
leave so much out; for instance,

when King David was aged and infirm,
and his advisors—themselves wizen men—

thinking to minister his flesh which "gat
no warmth" with the warmth of a virgin's breast, brought

Abishag, the Shunammite, to his deathbed,
nothing is said of this slip of a girl,

probably twelve or thirteen, given the custom of the times,
torn or sold out of her mother's house,

or what she must have felt, those all-too-fleshy fingers
gumming at her childish frock.

We are told only she was medicinal, a bitter herb ministering
to him at all hours, though the King "knew her not."

And God…? He's so quiet, it's as if she didn't exist,
as if He left the room, abandoning David and his virtue

to the paltry mechanisms of the flesh. But she, Abishag,
what happened to her, after being embraced

by the corpse of man and God? She must have been like these apricot trees
whose budding—a rush of whiteness and bees,

the living snowdrift of spring — is gripped by the last spasm of winter,
every petal, its intricacies shriven, freezing to mud, for which

we all stand about on this cold morning and lament
and lament and lament and lament.

2

Buddha in the apricot tree
is waving a multitude of arms, each bud,
a cape of snow on a temperate mountain, the opening
of a baby's mouth, the dicotyledon dance of becoming
an imperishable seed. Buddha in the apricot tree
is weaving a ladder to heaven out of perishable
sexual blossoms. A boy plucks a blossom
and scatters the petals in the street. A girl
plucks a branch from the tree and holds
it to her face, breathing deeply. There
is no serpent in the tree, just the awakening
of the branches — a galaxy of white stars,
each one with an ember of color still burning
at its core — the bees swirling in the air. Our desire,
only our desire, makes a heaven
of the apricot tree.

Fortune-Telling

Reading palms as if reading the world to come,
mund for hand, feminine, but also as *"a point of time,*
mood, humor, measure…," there is a condition
defined as having *"an excess of energy,"*
more dangerous than any poverty
of feeling or expression, the hand thick and fleshy
as a wedge of meat or wood—the mounts
of Venus, of the moon, and of the five fingers, so swollen
that they bear no whorls, no lines of birth
or scars of fate. Other palms may bear
fingerprints on the soft hills of Apollo,
fingerprints that confer the gifts
of Saturn or Mercury—gifts of tongues,
time, love, foreknowledge—as if the finger
of the god had pressed its talent
into the fetal palm forming
in the placenta, but these palms are blank
as the face of the god of annihilation, the excess
of oneself, of one's own will
or feeling, wielding a hand
like a paw or an instrument,
a driven thing. To hold such a hand
is to cradle a stone, a stone used
for erasing the adulteress
or the saint, a thick-skinned
stone full of the blood of another, prickly,
quick to take offense, flooded
with feeling. Once only have I held
such a hand and looked into the face
of the red god, the knotted brow
of Brahma, the slayer, his gaze
turning through the room.

Parable of Snakes and Stones

1

In the market, a girl asks her father
if she and her brother can have a candy bar.
"No!" he says loudly as he steers toward
the produce aisles. She barters with him
as Abraham bargained with God to save
the cities of the plain and the sweet impulses
of his own soul. Today, they're on sale:
buy one, get one free. "No!" he shouts. "But, but,
I'll pay you back with my own money, I
have a dollar or two at home." "No!" he yells,
leaving her among the sweets and the flowers,
turning his back as if she would never know
the mystery of his ways, until she gives up
and follows the fiery cloud of his anger
into the desert, forty years of his "No."

2

Who among you if your child asked for a fish
would give him a snake? The priest explains
to us, as if we were children, that in the Sea
of Galilee there were "fish that looked like snakes,"
as if the word "eel" would elude our grasp:
so busy with father and son, he says nothing
of or to the woman in line at the post office
who promises her crying daughter, "It won't be long,
just hold it. Wait! We'll go home, show your father,"
as if only a father could remedy or save.
Fear of future punishment adding to her
present pain, the child cannot stop whimpering,
tears running her face, as her mother waits
for her lot to be called. The girl nurses

her own hand, cradles it to her chest and turns
her face, in shock, to everyone, until
one of the clerks immediately understands
that the girl slammed her hand in a car door.
Her number called, her mother pays her
postage, saying, "I don't know how, how you
could do that, I didn't know you *could* do that."
While the clerk rummages for a Band-Aid, the girl
unveils her fingers wrapped in bloodstained
toilet paper as Christ unveiled His lance-pierced
side, His still bleeding sacred heart to some
medieval saint. All of us, clerks, customers,
mostly women, always present at the tomb,
rush to her, as if, beneath our wings, we could
shelter her, like some stricken suburb of Jerusalem,
but her mother is lost, more like Hagar
in the desert, waiting for some angel,
word from the Father. "Okay, we'll go home,
we'll put some ice on it when we get home,"
though she seems to be talking to no one,
her promises, aimless, provisionary, as she lists
from stone to snake, dry well to dry well.

The Mythology of Heavenly Messengers

I could see the black wings glistening on either side
of her wooden head and that the trunk

of her body, carved from a single cottonwood root,
had no arms with which to rescue any child

being drowned in the sacred waters,
as was the custom, so long ago, each spring.

But, even so, I wondered why the mother
of all kachinas was named "Crow Mother,"

because it seemed the Hopi would have hated crows,
plunderers of the blue corn, grown frugally in any crevice of rain.

When I heard that she was in charge of the whipper kachinas,
the ones who drove the children before them, with leather thongs

terrifying the reluctant and disobedient
into the center of the plaza, ringed by their frowning fathers,

I understood finally, remembering how in the desert, it was always crows
who first found the dead, taking the eyes,

then the tenderest parts of the body—Crow Mother,
the shining beak that preened and hopped in the rib cage of a child.

Those children came back as a flock of kachinas, feathered, bringing rain
to the corn, rising out of the sacrificial well, the navel of the kiva.

Caw—she birthed them into death, and, according to the custom—
gods came dancing out.

Saint John of the Cross

He is not here in Fontiveros, Spanish Nebraska
of his birth. The red brick granary fills
with nothing but wheat, and the empty plaza
has forgotten the name of Juan de Yepes,
grandson of Jews, though it contains a statue
of his alter ego, Saint John of the Cross.
Even bound by the thinnest of golden threads,
the soul's inexplicably bound. Leashed
in the cell, the whips of the holy friars
scourged him as he knelt, three times a week,
at dinner hour, nothing to eat but cruelty.
When he finally saw Christ, He was
falling toward him, His arms stretched back,
coming out of their sockets for love of him.

It's clear why he left Fontiveros —
his love for mountains conceived by this
dreary view — but no one knows how he escaped
from prison. Or why love finally drove
him back. Sick, he asked to be treated
in Ubeda, for he knew no one would cure him,
the bishop would curse him: he could die
inferior, die unknown, die suffering greatly.
Only love can heal us, opening our hands
to a darkness that we keep trying to let go...
How happy he was, always leaping free of the cell —
Fontiveros, Salamanca, Ubeda, the World —
singing softly, no longer having to tear out
the feathers that kept sprouting from his limbs.

The Making of Saints

A peasant girl who roots in mud
for an unfailing spring becomes one,
not because the trickle of water eventually
overfills the grotto, not because her neighbor's
baby, thrashing his limbs, on his back
in the desperate puddle, cries out with restored
health and life, not because a bonfire of crutches
will be left at the site which was originally the village dump,
not because anyone who stands beside the girl
can see the lady to whom she speaks, and not because
of her fervor which only grows as the laughter
swells around her, but because the girl will name
the Lady as the Immaculate Conception, on a day —
O careful scrutiny of the calendar! — just days before
the Pope in Rome announces the Doctrine
of the Immaculate Conception, a doctrine
that will be twin, hinge, foundation
to the new Doctrine of his own Infallibility,
and which this girl, digging in the mud of Lourdes —
the *dolt* of her class, *a very idiot* according to the sisters,
empty as the earth itself filling up with water —
will become the cornerstone of.

"A lonely man in his greatness"

Pius XII, who for some unknown reason
always hated flies, rotted in his coffin.
He who had been crowned with such ceremony,
glittering in a bejeweled, ascetic pose, had
the tip of his nose fall off while he reposed
in state. He who had such a delicate stomach
that trains of foodstuffs traveled with him
and yet who, as Europe starved, faced
every heaping plate as if *opening a warrant*,
who was so parsed, he said nothing of the Jews;
who *smelled of the absence of all scents*,
who lifted his arms in a gesture of *immolation*
and said nothing for the Jews, who had himself
filmed carrying a lamb on his shoulders, who
required that *no human presence should mar
his daily stroll in the gardens*, whose odor
of sanctity was antiseptic doused on his hands
and linens, from whom the workers hid
in the bushes rather than disturb the *pure white wraith*,
who would not sanctify those who smoked
or uttered a single curse, who would say nothing
to the Jews, rotted in his coffin. The doctor
who tended to his strange undiagnosed ailments
embalmed his body with a technique
that failed like the Concordant with Hitler,
though, in a sense, it was successful,
elevating the absolute power of the Pope,
as his coffin was elevated through the streets
of Rome. As the trinity of coffin, one nested
inside the other, passed from the caecum
of Saint Peter's, past the appendix of the archives,
to the colic streets, through the gates of Ileum,

the bowels of the city itself, strange noises,
of belches, flatulence, erupted from the corpse
of the Angelic Shepherd—like the earth
in many places in Europe, even in 1958
still rising and falling to the noises of death.

Ishmael Remembers Abraham

In life, he was so quiet, he often seemed dead.
Now, in death, he is loud
with life. His mouth is filling
the bowl again with nails. Translating
is as large as its contents. My arms
weakened, my shoulders are melting
at the stubbornness of it all.
His feet are growing more distant.
He continues to sand his nails.
Shadows resume flying into the house.
What do I know of my father?
He never gave me heartstrings,
only all that I could bear into that desert
where my mother was drowning in a well.

The Face in the Depths of the Desert

I wasted so much time
fishing at night, my anger
burning and anchored
to the railing of the houseboat,
while the lantern cast the rippling interstices
of my nets, snarled rods and lines,
onto the canyon walls of that dammed river.

My fingers aching from so many knots—
trying to thread back through the original loop—
I kept on casting, trying to retrieve
something formless, absolute,
from the halo on the water,
while only the dying silvery lives
heaped up around my feet or trembled on the stringer.

Only the arrival of the carp made me stop.
Those useless, undesirable, "trash fish"
that my father taught us to leave, gasping for air
on the bank, arrived like the embodied breath
of a dragon, each finned flame, interweaving
around, beneath, above one another—
the immeasurable

on every side of their bodies—not
just "above" or "below." Out of the mist of unknowing,
they came into view, merging then breaking away,
rooting in the bottom mud or rising to take with a tiny kissing sound
a dragonfly from the surface,
and the skin of the lake trembled
and swirled.

Signs and Wonders

1

In the shops around Chimayo, the bins
are full of miracles for sale, *milagros*
in the shape of whatever makes one moan—
in cheap tin or dear silver, a hand, a leg
from hip to toe, an ear, and even those pains
too hard to outline outside the body—
a failing eye, a twisted spine, an ache
within the breast. Constellations of groan
that shimmer when worn by pilgrims in search
of sacred mud. Yes, it's mud they swallow
or wear, hoping to leave their own ache
pinned to that wall, where a galaxy
of limbs orbits in endless thanksgiving
a gigantic sword-pierced Sacred Heart.

2

Though miracles can be undone. As in
Lima, 1845, when a mob stormed
the church and discovered their Christ
was no more than a life-size puppet,
his head bobbing upon the cross, being
pulled this way and that by a priest's fingers
behind the confessional screen. They burnt
that *little man*. For centuries, the tribunal
had turned to that wooden head—Christ alone
could grant some mercy at any human trial.
But he found no one innocent, set no one
free. Each time, his head, a cosmic *no*,
his eyes would roll back into his skull,
as if in death throes, his face spasmodic.

3

And restored, as when a cross was found
shining in the earth at Chimayo and named
in memory of the priest who had been buried
with it, so long ago, until the river washed
him free of its grip and left only the form
of suffering to illuminate the earth.
Originally, the earth was *tsimayo-pokwi*,
a sacred pool, its red mud, a remnant
of the Ancient Ones, until the puddle
turned to dust. Yet people keep coming
to eat of the earth or to smear its miracle
upon their crippled limbs. We never know
what god we worship. From the beginning,
we have been earth-eaters, our mouths full of mud.

If the Shroud of Turin Is a Fake

So what if the bloodstained linen never
rose, waving its arms about, and those feet,
pierced by a nail, never again strolled
that garden, crushing the aromatic herbs?
I don't care if this planet ever rolled
back from that tomb. It's the being crucified
that I believe in. Not the suffocating
of a rare beetle in a preservation jar,
but the dying as so many others dying,
or the way the living each morning rasp
their way up the stairs, as He Himself
enlarged the wounds in His feet—to rise
for one more breath, one more moment—
by standing on His own bones…

God, the Gardener

The *paradiso* of the bees and the hummingbirds
    withered to pods, pendulous, rattling
        on the stems. As the translucent
           husks dried, the seeds
               became more prominent,
                   visible even from a distance, gravid
                       souls swelling in the sheath until
                    they fell.

Like the beeweed, we will lose
    everything but the
        framework, our skeletal
           purgatory radiant with ice,
              glittering on the frozen
                 sword of the angel of exile, rising
                 again and again
                    out of the melting weight
                    of the snows.

By the time spring comes, if spring
    ever comes, the human heart will have been
        crushed so many times
           rising out of the weight of the falling
              then melting snows, or
                 torn back and forth
                   by such violent feelings
                      that All that connects
                         What is above the ground

to Whatever is below
    will have worked free of the earth.
        The knob that connects

the trunk of heaven
to the roots below
will be
exposed,
like the wrist joint
of a human hand
gripping, letting go.

The Writing on the Wall

to Alan

When the book returned to me
from the paralyzed hand, when
it brought back nothing to me,
I did not need to read its shaking script
like the handwriting of an ailing God,
scribbling on an already ruined
wall, to hear its message of woe.
I did not need to tear the envelope open
to find the *T* of that "Too sad"
shriven in a field. The brown shroud
of the envelope confessed all.
Splotched green, the message had drowned
on the way, caught in the downpour
of a weeping God who had washed away
any return address and any
name. I opened it anyway
because I heard a man's voice crying out
within it. Someone else, someone new,
caught in the book of the dead.

Bitter Herb

I had to lie down in the earth myself,
plowing the sand
with my belly, propelling myself
under the wire fence
that kept us apart. I'd stood there,
for a long time on the other side, just
clinging to a post, until the sheriff said
someone would have to cross over
and identify the body. Through
the gauntlet of the earth—the scrambling
weeds, the willows striking my shoulders
like whips—I crawled and bent
and shuffled until I was beside my brother—
his face as if someone had taken it apart
and put it back together in an awry
riddle of wood. Death was a riddle
to Gilgamesh when he went looking for a way
to bring his brother, Enkidu, back to life.
He was told to find *the plant
of opening*, a mysterious herb
that grew by the banks of a stagnant pond,
like this one, at the edge of a desert waste,
and was warned that it would prick his own hand
as he cut free its bitter root. On the way back
Gilgamesh stopped to rest and bathe;
as he drifted back into himself, full
of relief, reverie, and rescue,
a snake came out of the grasses
and swallowed the herb of eternal life.
But these waters, near where my brother lay,
were still and empty. The plant of opening,
rose-colored, ambrosial, did not shimmer

like a prism in the murky depths. My brother
had aimed at his own heart, not once,
but twice, firing down that pathway
of the soul. And the only sign
of a snake was his discarded skin.
When I said "Yes, that is
my brother, Clinton Seiferle,"
I heard the fingers of the dead snapping
around me. They would not let me touch him.
He was still evidence, the last witness
to the story they thought they would find
in the gleanings of his fingernails,
in his shirt as if shredded by a swarm of bees
from the powder burns, in the ground seething
with ants, the flies swarming and settling
upon him, his dead dog that lay at his feet.
He had come to the edge of that abyss
where fear came out of the water
and consumed whatever could have
brought him back. Three days later,
I'm the only one who comes back
to life, realizing that I'm still
wearing the same clothes, my jeans
prickly with nettles. As I slip out
of the black and stinging fabric, I find
the pockets are full of sand. How can
I give this earth to the waters? For touching
these fine grains, these sparkling abrasions,
it seems I touch all that remains
of the lost face of my brother.

Law of Inertia

We've all known those transfixed
a moment. The girl, so golden in fifth
grade, dulls out, bragging of being a local
photo-shop manager by faded sixteen.
More than mere accident; some moment
when time itself seems to conspire
on the self's behalf. A harried mother
grows perceptive and poised, one semester
of English assignments, then lapses back
into a lifetime of self-depreciatory jokes —
that she could have been a "good Mexican"
with her love of blue trim and pink light switches.
Some moment when love moves beyond
its usual allotments, when the air seems
full of species of affection that no one
has yet named, when a gesture or a word seems
to reach invisibly, deeply enough to quiet
the palpitating heart, when the teacher
trembles for the student on a motorcycle,
when the murderer lies down in the mercy
of words, when the boy who was thought
to be mute steps forth and speaks.
Some halting step, all we know of miracle,
a moment so fleetingly gone, briefly
elastic that then grows brittle and snaps,
as what tried to climb up the back stairs
of heaven's mansion falls back, caught
on the trellis, hemmed and hawed, snagged
and stunted to the gravity field, that
unforgiving inertia which we call "ourselves."

The Relic

All the way home, I kept thinking of the lost
finger of Saint Teresa, displayed
in the gift shop of a convent where she spent
most of her life being thrown by the devil
down the stairs or gripping the handrail
after communion, so others wouldn't see
how it took all of her strength to keep
her body from flying away. A wild hen,
a fighting breed, she still broods over Avila,
as if she could hatch that penurious flock
into God's generosity. Now as then,
they grasp and peck, scraping—too poor to mock—
God's cold stone nest. For pilgrimage,
all they have left is her finger, a relic

of her body—often disputed,
buried elsewhere, periodically dug up
for proof of incorruptibility. It was said
for centuries, she refused decay,
though at each exhumation, a little less
of her was left: a hand was taken for a monastery,
a splinter of sternum for the Empress,
and the peasants, well, took what they could get,
a woman bent to kiss her feet to bite
off a big toe. *"They go around crying
about the devil or longing for a sign,"*
she scolded, waving, perhaps, this finger,
though, probably, without this clot of green,
this emerald ring that makes one doubt

all vow of poverty... Is the digit
even hers at all, or that of some fuck-me

lady, thought lovely enough to stand in
for a saint's? If godliness requires
beauty, then her finger of insult—flung
at God after a horse bucked her into a stream—
you have so few friends because you treat them
so badly—has an afterlife of gem.
Life as a nun would be purgatory,
but better than an eternity in hell.
Yet it's her body that lingers in limbo.
A cloud of delicate mold—the halo
of God upon this earth, fine as an angel's hair—
clings to her finger, tries to call her home.

Face of the Leviathan

When I return home, the pond's a scene by Bosch.
For three weeks, in my absence, the apricots
falling from the trees have rotted in the depths,
and the sunny orbs that are still bobbing

on the surface move not to the current of water or wind
but to a congregation of innumerable worms.
A multitudinous mass, a writhing pulse,
some kind of soft white thing, pulpy, vibratile,

a maggot with a tail, which moves by pulsating
across the water, the long whip
of the flagellant sweeping, at random,
flagella spasming into crink or knot.

Beneath my flashlight, it's the face of a terrible deity,
a sun fallen and being eaten, a swarm beyond counting,
a mass, the size of a dinner plate, mouthing, eating,
defecating, breeding—whatever it is they do—

in that ungodly halo, writhing around a single
ripe apricot, its flesh dissolving, torn back
and forth in the water by their movement
as they twitch and burrow into one another.

In the morning, I go out like Arjuna in *The Mahābhārata*
to kill the endless horde. In the very roots
of the lilies, I see the tails rising up, air lines
floating up to the surface, plumb bobs of desire,

their heads and bodies buried in the wiry roots of the plants.
There are more of them than I imagined, even in the dark
repulsion of my dreams. They fill the pool
from rim to rim, challenged only by the equally numerous

mosquito larvae. The pool is anaerobic, a mass of sludge,
rotting apricot and lack of oxygen and what we have
brought the earth to, and only they could thrive
in this paradise. In their ability to quickly exploit

a favorable environment, the young ones thin as hair
and insubstantial as an individual sperm, the older ones thick
and full with what they've consumed, the worms seem
almost human. When I sift them like wheat from chaff,

their tails grip the wire screen
as anchorites once anchored their ragged forms
to desert spires. When I scoop them out and dash
them to the ground, they go off crawling, persistent

as pilgrims, leaving a trail in the wet ground for the rest
to follow. When I crush them into the weeds,
they begin drilling themselves into the roots
like nomads reaching the land of milk and honey.

I try to purify them, but they go on rising and falling
through the bleached water. I try to contaminate
them, but always a few, clinging to the refuge
of a crevice, manage to escape the poisoned drift.

All day we fight one another, and at evening,
a storm approaching, I survey the pond like a battlefield

and count on the fingers of my hands
the few still writhing on the surface.

Moved by curiosity, I scoop one up into my palm
and, seeing it so closely — as formless as I am, all appetite
and desire beneath my crushing fingers, a rubbery and persistent
self for all the formlessness of its being —

I am suddenly stung by love. Mother, father, sister worm,
all along I've been reading the wrong book,
the holy text of a sad and regretful God,
who exterminates whatever He cannot take into Himself.

When Leeuwenhoek found the "animalcules"
thriving in all falling rain, in pond water and in wells,
and in the human mouth, he peered through an eye
that he had made — his microscopes,

tiny pinheads of glass riveted together by brass —
and saw that these "minute, despised creatures"
were not bred of the filth of the world or spontaneously
generated from decay, but "endowed with as great perfection

in its kind as any large animal." Those forms
or something like them, aeons ago, writhing through primordial soup
became the colonies of our cells, sister
to our mitochondria, brother to our DNA,

and, now waiting in some exiled paradise for the fruit
to fall again from the tree, they are still God's first word
cast into the waters — *multiply, multiply* —
the first seeds of Being, of formlessness itself,

the golden egg of the father from which he himself was born.
In the center of the pond, twenty or so worms have wound
themselves together, their bodies the tiny white penes
of a vibrating wheel of unending

sexual congress, so I cannot tell
how they are linked, by mouth or anus,
tied together in a hub of desire, emptying
themselves into one another, all the protoplasm

streaming from one to another, in endless exchange,
like sperm linked to one another, or tiny pieces of living
intestine, all appetite and tail, until they hang limp, flagging
from the wheel, then revive again, corkscrewing

their way into the leviathan egg that the last apricot
has become, as brilliant
as our decaying sun, the universe exploding, a flagelliform spinning,
its petals infinite flesh.

VOICE
IN THE
WHIRLWIND

The City of Brotherly Love Is Neither

At the museum, when I turn the corner,
I'm cornered by a painting by Goya.
A blind man pries open the mouth of a boy
to grasp the scent of the bite of sausage
which the boy has just gulped down, singeing
his fingers on the sweet link that was being
roasted for his master. Caught in that grip—
one hand around his throat, the other
with two fingers chinked, grapple hooks
into his teeth—the boy's face is not satiated
but near death, eyes rolling back in his skull,
while the man's face, suffused with longing,
is just inches away, feasting on his breath.
So poverty has its blind expressions
and, crying from hunger, its notes, distinct
as Caruso's or Pavarotti's: out of all the cries
of which the human throat is capable—that gnawing
of the honeyless self, the drone of the empty
gut. So when I turn the corner at the Food Warehouse,
I'm cornered by the whine of a three-year-old passing
the lunch meat. Even his father, his scarecrow father
who bends to him with the voice of the wind
in an empty field, who asks if he wants
to carry the little red basket which holds
two or three things, seems to think he's crying
as children do, with unhappiness or irritation.
As his father drifts, like the blind man, past
the cases of what he can't afford, the boy
fights with the small basket, trying to carry
it and at the same time grasp the hot dogs
that slide about in its depths. When he's finally got
them, he drops his father with the basket—almost empty

now — and turning away, moves quickly down
the aisle, eight plump links in both hands,
his fingers tearing at the cellophane.

Biosphere 2

Oh, we hate the place from the beginning,
the pretension that calls the tasteless tacos
"a Southwestern banquet" and that tells us,
again and again, over interminable loudspeakers
that we're so lucky to be able to gaze into this glass coffin,
as if this pyramid glinting in the desert sun, its interior
divided into sterile plots representing "grassland," "desert," "ocean,"
were the equivalent of the original flowering—
the earth itself renamed *Biosphere 1*.
It's the international science fair, and only a few
are chosen. The brightest remove their shoes in a halo
of sterilizing light and are ushered into "the rain forest"
where a multitude of cockroaches, each the size
of a baby's hand, glue themselves to the glass, as if some longing
drew them back to the desert outside. The rest of the visitors drift,
as we do, into the orbit of the white phallic dome, guided
into a descending maze, promising an underwater view
of the ocean, though the path steers us inescapably
toward the gift shop where the stuffed
seal and sharks have more life than the "ocean,"
a surging sludge in a gray tank, where
a handful of convict fish swim in the tide
of a low-volume pump, its wires as exposed as a heart
in emergency-room repair. All around us,
the desert hums with the trajectories of jewel-throated
hummingbirds, the moths piercing the bells
of the yucca, the bees and wasps making
a paradise of the most ordinary *yes*.
Yet the tour guides insist the Biosphere is our real
future, that when we have exhausted the original,
we can move in here, this earth in a jar
made possible by science, for aren't we all

children of innovation, drawn here by science,
the scholarships, the glittering medals? And it's true
that as the light fades and we gather for the ceremonies,
some young faces are held up to us again and again like the two or
                                                    three orchids
blooming inside the Biosphere, the surrounding foliage stripped
away to display the enormous sexual blossoms, already perishing
from the flood beams, the sheer wattage of the illumination.
At the end of the evening (most of the children sullen
at never being called into the light), a piñata
(like the final course at a meal where most have starved)
is hoisted from a front-end loader. The size of a baby elephant,
the papier-mâché globe has been painted to resemble the earth —
crude continents of poster green, smears of oceanic blue.
As the loudspeaker invites *everyone, everyone,* to come forward,
Bolivian ballplayers take turns with bats, trying to split open
this facsimile of the planet. The children and sponsors rise to their feet
as the loudspeakers invite them forward, promising a taste —
T-shirts, candy, free passes, so many "other things"
hidden within the bulging crust. My husband warns me,
but I let our daughters go forward. As the piñata cracks open,
loud as a lightning strike, the crowd like a single organism,
an amoeba in the act of engulfment, pulses, then contracts:
even those at the far edges are swallowed up.
As my husband and I grab our infant son and step backward,
we see nothing but this surging formlessness,
and our two daughters disappear from view.
In a moment, they come running to us, their faces stricken
with being pushed to the ground, stepped on, barely able
to crawl out. As we flee to the car,
the air is full of rumor. *A girl was trampled to death.*
A boy had his legs broken. Someone was in a coma.

In the days afterward no one will ever say
what was sacrificed here, who perished
or remained forever crippled. A blackout
will follow in the local news, no official
announcement, no explanation why it was necessary
to create this arena of starvation, where so many
shining minds would rush to grasp at such trivial spoils.
Though as the ambulances coasted onto the grass, one after the other,
many people were still rushing forward, scrambling
for whatever was left upon the ground beneath
the shattered piñata, its skin torn away,
revealing an inner framework like the crushed spine
of some unspecified, living creature, gutted
and consumed, twisting in weird revolutions, hanging from the hook.

Galileo Was Finally Buried in the Body of the Church

except for the middle finger of his right hand,
exhibit iv.10 in the Florence Institute and Museum
of History of Science, listing
between a display of magnetic lodestones
and his portrait. Taken for a relic
by a disciple in the new faith of science,
in a new grail shaped like a planetary
orb of glass, stationary upon a pedestal
of alabaster — *This is the finger...*
which scanned the heavens and spanned
their immense space, though the elegant digit
has withered, tightening in the grip
of what is missing. *That wondrous instrument*
which pointed to new stars... now just
another false radius of the trajectory
of the self, Galileo Galilei, an idolatry
of the mind, as the withered finger begins
to resemble a miniature figure of Christ,
as if sculpted by Giacometti, the fingernail,
his shrouded face. Though, arching backward
as it does, mummified by time, the finger
resembles nothing so much as that gesture
recanting on any honking street outside —
fuck you, se muove, it moves.

Widow's Mite

*... he observed the crowd putting money into
the collection box.... one poor widow came and
put in two small copper coins worth a few cents.
He called his disciples over and told them:
"I want you to observe that this poor widow
contributed more than all the others.... They
gave from their surplus wealth, but she gave
from her want, all that she had to live on."*

MARK 12: 41–44

Whatever, the clerk says as she hands me the receipt,
and I don't know if she means whatever
I saved today at So-Lo, or the smell of blood
that she can't lotion away, leaking out
of the plastic-wrapped slabs of chicken,
or, perhaps, the impossibility of ever calling
anyone by his or her true name, or whatever
makes her reach out to pinch the shoulder
of the broom-pushing high-school boy
until he cries out, *What? What do you want?*
and she confesses, *Just to pinch someone.*
She keeps dipping her hands into a bucket
of diluted bleach as if like Pilate she could
wash away the cost of the accounting,
for, in truth, in this marketplace, we are all
counting the small change of our being:
the Vietnam vet in his battle fatigues
who keeps weighing his wallet against
the price of bits and ends of bacon
and two packages of red calf liver,
the teenage mother balancing a bag of chips
and a bottle of soda against milk and bread,

the widow digging in her purse for her last mite,
so many souls with broken zippers, trying
to shrug off the cost of this dearest of Sundays.

Modus Operandi

You were never to consider the worm
itself, drowning upon the hook, in a drift
of river or lake, or how it felt
when the barb punctured its body
at three or four strategic points... coiled
tightly around the metal, so it would survive
again and again your casting into the distance,
the falling through the air, the shock of striking
the surface. The idea was to make the worm
last as long as possible, though extending its life
was extending its suffering, so you could rethread
its brown vibrant length as it became slack, pale,
and waterlogged, carefully as a rich man threading
his way through the eye of a needle, even sometimes
managing to salvage enough leftover from the mouth
of a trout to use the worm again. Mud puppies
dredged from stock ponds, shimmering minnows,
baby frogs, crawdads, grasshoppers leaping
on the hook—all were means to an end: a fish
in the pan, an afternoon's art or recreation,
an exercise of skill, an idea of how to work
a stream or pond, and it became a way of looking
at things, a way of being. You remember this
when you hear on the evening news that a man
in a nearby town who molested six toddlers
began by using his own three-year-old daughter—
her wanting to play with other children—as *bait*.

Every Consecrated Head

It's the hair that makes me cry, when my daughter
describes long-distance how they made her lover
cut his hair, the dreadlocks sacrificed
for his brother's wedding, and how
his mother seemed so warm as she manipulated
him into the shearing, and how he cried
in the barber's chair. It is the hair
that made love a philistine. That made
a child into a Samson who refused to cry
when her mother jerked out the snarls.
That made the cowboys in the '60s catch any
longhaired boy on the Laramie streets
and cut away his glory and his strength
with sheep shears, leaving his skull a bloody
patch. It's the hair of the Lamb of God
that makes us worth more than a flock of sparrows—
every hair on your head has been counted,
so do not be afraid, but it's the hair on the head
of one in Gehenna *who can destroy*
both body and soul. It's the hair that made Medusa
the *lovely, the lively locked,* and it's the *full head*
of hair that makes a woman *a horror* unveiled
before Saint Paul. It's the lock of the beloved,
where the last kiss flutters like something caught
in a net, still tremulous, alive. It's the hair
of childhood trimmings kept in a cedar chest,
or in the medicine bag that a Peruvian child
clutched when left as a sacrifice. It's the bale
that no one knows what to do with—the tresses
falling and falling, now molding in the museum.
It's Rosh Hashanah, the Jewish New Year,
and listening to the account of the shearing,
it's not the hair that makes me cry.

Toledo

The synagogue of Samuel Ha-Levy
is full of the laughter of God. He laughs
ha ha in the nave of larch wood, relieved
to be so free of images, no longer forced
into limbs. He laughs in the Psalms of David,
written into the walls, still dancing naked
before the niche, empty of Ark. He laughs
and Samuel laughs with Him. Samuel who died,
being tortured, his dignity the hidden
treasure of which he would not speak… The Holy
of Holies of Samuel Ha-Levy forced
to become the Transit of the Virgin,
the Jewish Quarter made into a cloister,
then a barracks, a warehouse, and *ha, ha,*
a time came, when the Virgin vanished too.

And most of the saints in Spain
are the lost children of the Jews.

Bitter Fruit

For years I didn't know what to call them.
Each thing in my childhood was given
just one name — "walnut," "hazelnut," "pecan" —
but I couldn't say "nigger toes." I couldn't
get a grip on the bony ridges; the brown
triangular shells never seemed to fit
the nutcracker's silver jaw. Every
Christmas and at Thanksgiving, untouched,
in the cut-glass bowl, that name fastened
upon them and us made their sweetness
forever inedible. Lying for months
on the kitchen table, they could have been God's
toes, severed from His body and our language,
the fossilized fruit of some terrible tree.

Singing "eeny meeny miny moe, catch
a nigger by the toe," the fruit, my mother
used to say, never falls far from the tree.
My daughter says I should not say "picnic."
It sounds like such a lovely word — picnic
hams, picnic in the woods, the snow picnics
my father liked, spreading a cloth in a drift —
but has a terrible root — "to pick a nigger"
for a lynching, shortened to "pick-a-nig"
when everyone would ride out for a Sunday
of lunch and lynching. She just learned this,
while visiting another country. Stunned and silent,
we drive on. We will have to find another
language, if we want another world.

My Spanish Children

In my mother's home, my daughters
are little *Spanish* girls—like the nice
Spanish woman who, years ago, saved
me and my baby brother from the hail, running
out of her house, holding out a blanket
over his soft spot, when the stroller wheels
caught on the curb. So I hoped in Spain
my children would feel some homecoming,
but no look of welcome met my daughters
on all the streets of Spain. Matrons, my mother's
age, stopped short, with the eyes of Franco,
inspecting the indigenousness of their shoes.
Only gender made one native. In Madrid
when my two-year-old son wanted onion,
smiling waiters brought him a whole one,
as white and round as an American softball,
then quartered it with a single cut—the slash
of a sword knighting his shoulder, the pungent petals
of patrimony spreading upon his plate.
In Avila, when my daughter wanted strawberries,
the waiter held out his empty hands, then
brought a bowl of withered bananas,
which cost more pesetas than I cared to figure
into dollars and which no one would eat.
On the "sun" train, leaving the country, we
went reluctantly to the "free" breakfast,
expecting a slab of bread for the boy,
and a small fortune for the rest of us
to be able to wash it down. But, instead,
there were trays, one for each child—
orange juice, croissants, *pain au chocolat*—
and another family with tousled hair.

When the woman smiled at my daughters,
it came home to me that we must have crossed
the border—sometime while we were sleeping,
our bones jostling in the narrow bunks, our hearts
jangling like pocket change in God's uneven hand.

Homophobia

I could say that discovering such ugliness
in a friend is like standing on my own porch,
barefooted, ready to jump into the sweet grass,
still soft with spring newness, and finding coiled —
its outline broken by fractals of sand — the blunt
venomous head of a prairie rattler,
lying in wait, striking out at whatever
comes within range of its desire or fear.
Throwing itself forward, the snake
would be as certain of its normality as my friend is,
coiled around the memory of the man who died,
rattling with indignation at the news
that he died of AIDS, and I, I could be the mouse,
frozen with timidity, having blundered
on an exceptionally beautiful morning
into this toxic stare, struck dead on the spot,
the hypodermic lullaby poisoning my conscience
as much as muscles of my throat and heart. But
the snake is beautiful, those diamonds etched
along its spine as newly green as the fragrant sage,
and the mouse, the mouse being swallowed
would become of use, its cells, mother
and father of new snakeskins, and I could turn
back, refrain from jumping off the step, and the snake
would slide into the grass, its body a long sigh
breathing itself away, leaving me to thank heaven
for such a glimpse, and such a narrow escape.
The snake would not, as my friend does,
keep flinging itself at a dead man, talking about
how repulsive it must have been, how shocking
to imagine the lovemaking of two people
of the same sex, though she keeps imagining

it again and again. As if she held her soul
in an artificial grip, forcing its jaws open
to the naked drip and chill—though a snake,
so pried upon a petri dish,
would be milked of all its poison.

The Laws of Patrimony

All the firstborn—bloody, envious Cain,
sadly persistent Esau, besotted
Lot—know that he who works and works and works
his father's farm does not necessarily inherit it.
So my grandfather left whatever was left
of the fields in the silos to his youngest
son who had already bankrupted
the farm. And while the oldest son cursed,
my mother and her sister began fighting
over the surviving unmatched cups
of the wedding china. Yes, it was love
they longed for, always divided among them
like a torn and bloody coat—their hearts
on the altar of begetting, smoldering, unburnt
offerings to the Father who kept turning away.

The Custom

Gravied, sliced
down to the bone, every year
all that's left of the Thanksgiving
feast is the wishbone. Stained
the color of tea or rain seeping
into wood, it could
be beautiful, a singular harp
from which no one
has learned to coax
a tune, or an ivory white
bow of stars that never shot
a wounding shaft
but, instead, impelled
a feathered being into the air,
a hinge for the drumming
of earthly wings. But
the custom of the breastbone
is that only two of you can fight
over this good fortune,
only one of you can win,
so some Esau plucks the wishbone
from the carcass, some Jacob grabs
the other end. Sometimes the bone
tears and twists apart
as slowly as the strings
of DNA that bind you together,
the long fibers unraveling
in your opposing grips;
other times already brittle,
it snaps like the retort
of a branch breaking
from the cursed fig tree

or the jawbone with which Samson
slew so many Philistines.
Except for that one year,
when your mother hung
the disarticulated blessing to dry
in the kitchen window,
then, painting it red, transformed
the hollow endoskeleton into a small sleigh
for a velvet-coated Santa Claus,
his cheerful gaze steering blindly
through a decade of Christmases,
it has been the custom to fight
over the bones. You've always tried
to be the first to grasp
the better end, you and your
Cain or Abel torquing
across the kitchen table,
using the weight of your bodies
for leverage, until one of you
is left, triumphant, clutching
luck's fat knuckle, the other
its splintery end.

Fear-Biter

It wasn't your brother who kept that coyote
on a chain, slumped in the desert sun,
sadness leaking out of it as it dribbled
the weak boundaries of its territory, marking
the trail it had circled so many times, caught
in the wheel made by its own fretting
against the chain. No, your brother was
the coyote itself, at least in those moments
when no one was watching, and the creature
could imagine itself free of even the finest
of tethers, and it would shake out
the thick ruff of its being, its resplendent fur,
each hair to its follicle and root shimmering
with all the gradations of the multicolored earth.
Your brother's friend had trapped and killed
the creature's family, then raised it as a pet, solo,
useless among the heelers and shepherds, though
your brother took you to that farmyard so like
your grandfather's and all the farmyards
where he had worked—exhausted, trampled,
mud-packed earth, cluttered with the gutted parts
of tractors, the implements of caging
and butchery and for pulling calves out of the womb—
for he wanted you to see the coyote,
that strange avatar trapped in the yard,
an orphan as resplendent as your brother and just
as weirdly bedraggled and cringing from what
he was shackled to. The way the coyote
hunched over, hackles rising at any approach, lips
curling back from any gesture of the human,
was the way your brother learned to tremble
in an ancient schoolyard, when a ring of boys,

holding hands, ran toward him, as if in welcome
and instead fell upon him and began to beat
the hell out of him, until he would not, would never
back down, but charged forward, always leaping up—
the rest of his life tearing at the throat of his own fear.

The Housewarming Gift

My sister came bearing
the ceramic leopard I'd admired in her house,
      a new plant rooted in its hollow back, a tree
          blanketed with miniature red
              and yellow peppers, a lovely
                 poisonous cloud.
The color of the leopard was all wrong;
      the peppers could not be eaten.
          Yet I threw open gladly
              the doors of my new house
              and welcomed
her family, our sister Rachel, our mother Mary,
      as if to some sacred feast,
          the air rich with the scent
              of wine and roasting meat,
                 as if the leopard
were a picturesque pet
that would ask nothing of me.

It took a week for the whiteflies to appear,
hundreds hatching out of the soil of resentment,
      the porcelain sweating
          with stolen honey.
              In their immature forms, the bright green
                nymphs colonized
the underside of every leaf.
      Then, winged,
          a white and fluttering drift, their bodies
              like grains of salt poisoning the fields,
              they became
a scattering
      multitude, almost invisible,

like dust motes swirling in sunlight,
         or the mote that is only visible
                  when lodged in another's eye.
Finally nothing was left of the plant but the knot
of root like a buried fist clenching

its clump of negation,
and the trunk like a spindle rising
         from an ancient curse.
                  No matter how many cleansings
                           of Clorox or clouds of poison rain,
                                    the whiteflies always came back, surviving,
persistent as hatred or malice
         that wedges itself into the smallest cracks
                  of an apparently serene surface:
                           a face smoothed into pleasantries,
                                    ineradicable,
recurring like the resentment
         that Nietzsche saw spinning the wheel
                  of Christian life. Given the name of suffering—
                           "Mary" for "bitter root"—
                                    my sister would have done anything
to shine in our father's eyes, though what I envied
was how she bathed

in the eternal warmth
of our mother's gaze.
         Haloed in sunlight,
                  beneath the clothesline, she colonized
                           the kingdoms of the lawn
                                    with plastic soldiers

and defeated my brother
    so quietly, plotting
        with such stealth
            that my mother pointed to her
                as the very image
of goodness. As if
    passivity were goodness,
        as if the appearance
            of peace were
                Peace.
I should have known that one who claimed to want nothing
but to be

a rocking horse would become
a sender of wooden horses, a dealer
    in plundered pots, a subterfuge
        of broken angels, bearing
            the unending gifts:
                malice, envy, despair...
The whiteflies that invaded my new garden
    had plundered her home
        for decades, every transplant
            curdling. And, five years later,
                on any morning, I am still battling
the yellowed leaves, the branches sticky
    with the leak of their own lives.
        In the garden, the past lives on
            in the whiteflies, swarming
                like dust in a whirlwind,
like the dust of the grinding wheel
to which Samson was leashed in Gaza,

like the dust in which the accusation is written,
like the dust that throws the first stone, like the dust
    in which the one who keeps vigil
        lies down and goes to sleep,
            until the right hand
                knoweth not
what the left hand
    doeth. Here, every morning, I think of
        my sister and the lost paradise
            of childhood:
                in that ruined kingdom,
vengeance grows wings,
    and rises up
        in forms as numerous
            as the angelic hosts
                to drain away
the sweetness,
even the sweetness of the heart.

In the Village Where You Were Born

To every visitor she introduces her family
by pointing to this photo where she is a baby
in a circle of infants, her mother
and all the mothers in the ancient village
where she was born, and where, as children,
they caught great blue dragonflies and on fine
strings flew their iridescence through the air.
It's all vanished now, the living kites,
the ancient *madres*, the village itself,
and the blond baby to whom she always points,
and who died in the first year of life
from all those recessive genes. *Qué bonita!*
she says, at seventy — *That skin so light!*
Only that lost cousin, her hair a halo
against adobe walls, proves the family
was truly Spanish — conquistadores not slaves.

The Mortgage

The house goes up like possibility.
A cloud caught in its doorway. Two-by-fours
framing the sky. But then it fills with glass,
bricks, plywood, insulation, and shrinks
into itself. Solid as the grave, shrouded
in tar paper. Not so "grand," not a "mansion."
But the cheap minimum for this lot.
The new owners come and go, their vision
reaching no farther than their arms, fixed
on the molding, the skeletal stairs. They do not
look at the sky or into a neighbor's face,
though we hear them at night, announcing grandly
on the other side of the fence, "a party
and play area," in the backyard that is
exactly the width of a dog run.

"Animal People"

"Skincrawlers" the Navajo call those who slip
into animal form. So when the wolf hybrids
howl at one in the morning, you hear the voice
of your neighbor, caterwauling when drunk,
or when the setters bay with that horrible
choking bobble-babble, it could be his wife
trying to swallow her husband's prattle.
Your brother can lock up his heeler, but then
he's the fear-biter at dinner, snarling
at the finger-snapping of BLM or NRA.
The mare, fretted and driven, could be your sister,
bit-biting, flinching at the leap. Remember
how at goat shows the losers would kick every
lower-than-second-place udder, no matter
how swollen or full? All night in the row
of trailers, you could hear their voices throwing
buckets of shit at their own children, while
in the barn, the winning animals would collapse
into the straw like empty and exhausted vessels.

Voice in the Whirlwind

I know about the birth of the mountain
goats, have kept vigil for the birth pangs
of the does, have numbered
the months that they must fulfill
and calculated the time of their bringing forth.
They crouch down and bear their young;
they deliver their progeny in the desert,
but I do not know why you have done this,
why the earth cries out and is afflicted,
why it cries out as if in labor
and does not bring forth.

In the high mountain meadows of Utah,
deep in the green with the rich texture
of newly printed money, the lambs
struggle to their feet, each spring,
their legs growing a little shorter,
the shanks diminishing, as the breed
is genetically engineered for its haunches,
so that one day nothing will frolic
in these pastoral scenes but
a rounded rump, a chine of living
meat.

I asked the beasts to teach me,
I lay down among the grasses,
I asked the birds of the air to tell me,
the snakes and the bright lizards
to instruct me, I cast my understanding
into the waters of the oceans,
the rivers, and the lakes,
and asked the fish of the sea to inform me,

but they could not tell me why
you have done this.

In the fields of Eastern Europe, in the pastures
sown with abandoned mines,
the fireflies flicker every night
as they hunt for the sweet sexual
scent of TNT, the land mines
emitting a faint odor
that the fireflies are drawn to
as once they were drawn to
the male and female of their own kind.

My days have passed away, my plans are at an end.
Such men change the night into day;
when there is darkness, they talk of approaching light.

Another phosphorescent
glow, a pheromone of longing,
now trembles in their cells
so they wish to mate with dynamite.
Created in the shape of our desire
to locate the hidden mines
that we buried in the earth,
they are tiny whirlwinds of agitated light
gathering above the earth, fathering
nothing.

Because you could not look into the faces of the wounded
without believing only in the wound.
Because you could not look
into the face of the wound,

even the wound you yourself have inflicted,
and love it. Because you could not
look into the face of the wound
without wanting to erase
its puzzling gaze. Because you believe
only in your own necessity
to exist, because the universe
owes you this, even the birds
of the air, the creatures moving
upon the face of the earth, and
those in the depths of the sea, I have turned
away from you, I have spit you out...

In upstate New York, in a sterile
laboratory, a special breed
of white mouse is growing
a human ear in the skin
on its back. The whorl
rides upon its spine, as the tender
lobe, the spiral of human flesh,
takes shape like a fetus
in the placenta
of the mouse's almost transparent
skin. The mouse is pure,
a genetic X, its skin
like the thinnest
of veils, revealing
the ear caught in the net
of its veins. As it moves through the
cage, the mouse stops, tentatively
turns toward the glass, as if it could hear
the voice of the whirlwind on the other side

with that human ear pricked
on its back, listening, listening…

I know that you can do all things,
can stretch out your hand and give
an ear to a boy who was born with none,
can stretch out your hand
and all the firstborn will be born without limbs,
can send the creatures of the air
to find the weapons which you have hidden
in the valleys and in the mountains, can feed
the hungry with food that will not sustain them,
can heal the sick so that they bear
the heart of a monkey, a pig's liver, the kidney
of a murdered boy, can make the dying outlast
the organs of their own body, can transform
a desert into a garden, and make a desert of the earth,
and no purpose of yours can be hindered,
and that your wonders are infinite,
beyond number. I have dealt
with things that I do not understand,
things too terrible for me,
which I cannot know.
I have heard of you by word of mouth,
but now that I have seen
how you truly are,
I tremble with fear and sorrow
for all that lives and breathes.

Between the Imagined and the Real

It's harder to imagine mercy than to imagine death. Yet we must
body forth that bodiless reality, no matter

how many times we wake up in the middle of the night,
or think in the park: if this city were sixteenth-century Paris,

or London in the seventeenth, entering by any
fate, we would have passed the gallowed dead

hanging from the gates, their gazes
like dull bruised flags of warning.

Entire civilizations have pleasantly strolled by cages
containing the remnants of human beings. What I don't know

is whether we would have been used to it—
as little, as much—as we are now to

the homeless man clawing at his own eyes,
muttering "Forgive me, forgive me…"

to whoever passes by. I remember the story
of that poet who grew up in a country

where people were still publicly hanged
and how he said that, strolling beneath the forked limbs,

they called those hanged
the *bride* and *groom*.

The Argument

I cannot believe in the saccharine
comforter, the eyewash of light,
        that All,

regardless of will or desire, suffocate in heaven's wing.

Even in my father's decrepit King James,
stolen from one of his many wives,
its binding flaking away from having been read too much,

      I find no word
of that vague realm.

        Our Father
        who art in Heaven, etc.

Only the divine roosts
at those altitudes, like rookeries
of angels on an unscalable cliff,

        and what's left to us

is the body at some unsettled date,
rising to everlasting
        and on
and on and on and on.

So where did it come from,
this plump realm of cherubim, where
an aged Jehovah's Witness who always
wanted to play the piano insists
she'll be playing "Clair de lune"?

The priest at the funeral will speak of nothing else
but those wings waiting, hung upon their hooks, tailored suits

in a clothing store we never expected
to afford. O dim realm,

I do not think
the dead are in heaven. My brother

who killed himself on Sunday
is not today caught up in an angel's wing.

Nor would he have wanted to be.

I sit with him in the swamp each morning, by the sad fact
of his torn and discarded flesh;

neither of us says anything. It's all too clear—
the light of the body

is all we know
of paradise.

MY
MOTHER'S
HIP

My Mother's Hip

O the mothers, the mothers...
FAUST

1

What she wanted most was not to hear
her own hip and socket being torn away.
Yet the doctor couldn't offer oblivion,
just the epidural's numbness, enough drugs
so she would not care. Drifting in and out,
she would hear the crack of bone and hammer
but not feel the injury as her own. *Ha, ha, ha,*
she wakes, laughing at a doctor's joke.
But to me, it's the story of her life,
the elixir that they gave her, just another
dram of limbo, the water of forgetfulness
that only the dead are meant to drink.
From that first taste on an abortionist's bed,
she's been drunk: her body, not her own.

2

Surely the unwanted child is older than the gods,
being their first incantation, poured into a manger
as bitter herbs are crumpled into a cup of wine
or as a chalice of God's blood was poured out
upon a naked hill, his tiny hands, her tiny feet
unable to fly away, no matter how they beat
the air. So, in the Greek myth, Psamathe
denied the existence of her son, born
of the god Apollo, to appease her father, the king,
and he, recognizing his own features in the child's,
ordered him devoured by dogs. In the only remedy

the myth could ever allow, she and her son
were transformed into dogs, strays forever
protected by a god's mercy, freely roaming
the streets, except for that one day—*Kerophontis*,
dog-killing, god-killing day, when their descendants
were ritually slaughtered. So we hear the dog pack
of our own hearts howling on every distant hill—
every unwanted child, every unacknowledged mother—
reminding us of a sweet baby whose name meant only
"suffering came into the world."

3

Now I've nursed my mother back to health,
I know what my birth cost her. Then as now,
she had to be knocked out, in labor
for hours, made into scaffolding, her legs
spread in horrifying angles, so I
—umbilical knotted around my throat—could be
extracted by the forceps that shaped us both.
Her body wouldn't let me go. No wonder
she could not forgive me. Among the Maya,
women who died in childbirth instantly
entered Paradise. She lived on in limbo.
In her arms, I must have arrived less a baby
than aftermath, like this arthritic hip cast
aside, something torn from her—not *hers*.

4

The left hand knoweth not what the right hand
doeth, yet my brother knew the doctors were carving
when he shot the deer, then tracked its bloody
spoor for hours through the falling snow. Like Esau

hunting as his father died, all he wanted
was the mess of pottage, not the crowning
rack. In medieval tapestries, a deer
was an image of a *soul*, so mercy,
too, escaped him when, in a freezing
canyon, the deer finally slipped away.
Wistful, now, he hopes the doe — *like our mother* —
will recover in her snowy bed… somehow,
out of his sight, beyond death's blessing.

5

Among the long-lost relatives, over
the splintered wishbone of a roasted chicken,
on the eve of her own going under, she rattles
on about my operation at age five.
She wants it clear how imperious a child
I was — in post-op, refusing to speak,
as I pointed to whatever I wanted:
her father almost died on the snowy
roads because he went searching for ice cream
for her torn throat; she ate fifty Popsicles;
she was terrified of the gas mask
that the nurse slipped onto her face;
passing out, she kept crying: "Rock-a-me,
Mommy, rock-a-me, rock-a-me." All day

my husband and I cooked this lovely
feast — sweet rolls, potato salad, a golden bird —
for this forty-year reunion. Yet here
we are choking down this cold ancient dish.
My voice sounds just like hers, so when she mimics
me, it could be the lost voice of her own

childhood that she invites her siblings
to mock: herself, the casualty, who ha-ha's
upon this table, curdling among the meringues.
"Grandma," my daughter says into the dead
quiet, her voice, new rain, falling softly
on that ancestral farm, its bankrupt silos.
"Grandma… that's not funny, that's just sad…"

6

The goddess of mercy delivered every child
into the world, sitting on a lotus flower
that drifted on the lake where the nine goddesses
of becoming blessed the child's suckling,
breathing, weaning—so many gestures
of kindness flowing out of the Milky Way.
Lost now like the ancient names of the stars,
our Mother who was once in Heaven
as in the Earth, hallowed be her name,
of whom I remember nothing. It was not my mother
but *her* mother who rocked me into being,
the one who rocked my mother into a kind
of living death rocked me into endless life,
cradling me in the scent of lilacs. The self?
No more than the smallest shape, coiled
warm upon a breast, rocked by something
I could not yet sing—*la la la la la*…

7

Oh, she said, she only pretended to play,
strumming the guitar to a single chord,
at four, at five, *get along little dogies*
and *yippee yo ki-yay*, but thought she heard

real music, so when her mother and father
pointed out that she was playing nothing—
just strumming, "like a retard," her voice out
of tune—it was real shame she fell into.
She stopped playing her heartstrings. So full
of white noise her father wouldn't let her
into the milking barn; her silence made the cows
too nervous. The rest of her life, a joke
like the shadow that she ran shrieking from,
she became an orphan in the house of ridicule,
slowly adopting its native tongue.

8

Äpparas, a Lapp word, and I've never
been to Finland, though I know how frigid
the lap is in which a child can never
lay her head. *Äpparas*, when a child's ghost
haunts the landscape of its death without
proper burial rites, and since the landscape
can be a mother's flesh—*She was never
mine.* The firstborn could never be defeated,
flushed as he was down the drain, or ever
exorcised, buried as he was in a mind
already full of cold spots, the phantoms
of the mothers. So many mothers disinherited,
so many mothers, never born. So many daughters
who could never be her beloved, who
could never *be;* instead, buried in a vase
in the shape of an animal, under the stone of her gaze.

9

The violence of men, the malevolence
of women; it's not the mother alone,
but her mother who abandons her at the abortionist's
door, and her father pacing the hotel room
for whom her mother forsakes her
at the abortionist's door, and the abortionist
herself, a "Spanish woman," *the only one
who shows any kindness* while carefully
packing the uterus with cotton to drive
the fetus out, and the phantom of the father,
and the priest who runs from the confession,
and all those relatives, who when you arrive—
almost stillborn in 1951—will love and hate you,
being as you are, without knowing it,
from birth, both redemptor and ghost.

10

I looked into the rearview mirror, and saw
that my mother, somewhere along the way,
had turned into the stiff white Goddess of Death—
a pale limestone effigy wedged between
my unhappy children. *What's wrong?*
I'd ask. *Are you okay?* But she never answered,
gripping her large pink purse as it thumped
between her legs. Her body, caught in the torque
of some powerful claw, seemed diatomaceous earth,
a white bitterness, a fossilized cloud. I blamed
the car seat and the door, thought it might be
a mini-stroke, microbursts in the brain, but, no,
she was fine. We went on. *Didn't I remember
it had always been like this?...* Suddenly

she'd turn to me, her gaze burying me
in a vase in the shape of hedgehog or frog.

11

What regenerates first is shell. Her look
of Jell-O, quivering in the mauve molds
of the hospital cup and vomit basin, healing
and gelling to crab sheen, her polished carapace.
When I saw her sitting in a chair, eating
like a human being for the first time
in days, and she chomped down my hello
to dip her roast beef into the *au jus*,
I knew that she was resurrected. Proud
as a lobster waving its one good claw,
she wore the "me first" exoskeleton
that I'd always known, and for the first time
in my forty-eight years, I was happy, oh,
so happy, to be met by her beetlelike stare.

12

Light rain in the park of recovery.
I help her find her footing, steer her clear
of the small treacherous puddles. I'm glad
for the rain falling and falling upon us.
All those years I painted the same image—
a fetus curled in an acrylic ocean—
I thought it was myself, nearly stillborn,
perhaps my twin, the lost knot of tissue
my mother unraveled in my carrying,
and, finally, my long-lost brother. But
I know now, it was my mother's soul I saw—
my mother trying to be born, my mother

who at sixteen must have felt the last stone
falling into place, while her face became
a reconstructed, sacrificial altar,
and her spirit flew away. In tiny shrines,
the Japanese honor the unborn by pouring
water over altar stones, so I pray
the rain falling and falling upon us
may be the water that births us both.

13

THE PALM RESCUED FROM YOUR MOTHER'S HOUSE

She
had drowned it
with her tears
and kept it in the dark
of a forgotten room. Because
she could not bear
to throw out
the trunk like a stub
of umbilical cord, she gave it
to me, and, on my table,
in sun-drenched light,
it began to grow,
inch by inch, unfurling
layer by layer, growing
as tall as a young girl
filling the room
with seven veils
of green. Each morning,
on my way to work, I notice how
beautiful it is, how full

of life—like Salome in the corner,
                beyond her mother's bidding—
diligently working, reattaching its head to
                its body, its body to the earth.

14

Always I have been officially firstborn,
the one destined to perish at the threshold,
at the passing of the Angel of Death,
so I take responsibility, wear the mantle,
drive my mother to the knives at five AM,
while my sisters come in like Esau, late
in the morning, want to eat, take a nap,
yet we all know the doctor will prefer
to address their bucolic blondness, will avoid
the riddle of my stare. For in truth, I am
her Jacob. Because my mother never
sang me to life, I sit here and sing. Because
she never sang me to sleep, I sit here
and sing, to sing her awake.

THE
SACRIFICE
TREE

At the Beginning

of the ruins, we inhabit a sky full of cries too numerous and varied
to be identified. And what would we
call them?

The bird that cries like a man...

The bird that buzzes
with the voice of the locust pinched in the thumbs of a branch, the bird
with the voice of a whistle made of a human thighbone,

one last breath... just before
it breaks? The bird whose periodic
cry is a bright thread among the bullrushes...?

These warbles, clicks, cries of surprise
throng us with a language
we do not understand:

our own tongue, the lost voice
of our fathers meeting our mothers so long ago,
the voice of whatever calls
us into being...

Archaeological Record

When King Olaf was converted
to the sign of the cross,
it was by the Proof
of a sparrow flying through
the suddenly stricken great

> *The Sarajevo excavation has unearthed*
> *a tomb containing the fully articulated skeleton*
> *of one man. Several artifacts*
> *were found with him; of most interest*
> *is a bronze helmet with a stiff plume*
> *that appears to be made of horsehair*

hall, from one end to
another, from one door
to the next, so Brief
is human life.
Is it yesterday

> *and which resembles the helmet*
> *of the Philistines, "the sea-faring*
> *Peoples" depicted on various*
> *Egyptian friezes, hundreds of them*
> *defeated, a rope linking their necks*
> *as they are led away by a single thread*

or are the ships setting sail for Troy
tomorrow? The stones
of the city are still smoldering
with a fire that could not be
extinguished,

of fate. As already noted,
the Helmet of the Philistine
resembles the helmet of the
Achaeans who destroyed Troy,
and other armor found with the corpse
includes the characteristic greaves,
breastplate, short sword...

the walls consumed
in a fire so hot
that it made whatever
was made of earth — the bricks
of every house and temple, the paving stones
of every street—

 which may elucidate the origins
 of these warring peoples, for even though
 archaeomagnetic or carbon dating has not
 yet been completed, this "Adam"
 appears to be the oldest specimen
 yet unearthed, his armor, the earliest
 example.

catch fire and burn, and when everything else
had been consumed, the ground
caught fire and the earth, the earth itself,
began to burn.

The Excavation

Digging, on the fourth day, you find a stone
feather, an angel's wing, torn from the house
of the king. In the postclassic age, the people
ransacked the kingly lintel for the threshold
of their house. They went into the inviolate temples
and took what they wanted. Perhaps,
they could still hear the wings rustling, fixed
and trembling to the frame of heaven, like a living bat
nailed to a doorway, still trying to take flight,
to return to the cave of origins that in a classical age
was also the door to the sky. *Whose history
has power over me?* you ask when you wake
in the morning from nightmares of Mayan gods.
Whose wing is that brushing by? you ask,
not sure if the fever is your own or the sun's,
as you hear that someone else, a village girl,
died in the place where you were standing
just a moment ago. When the villagers stole
that divine wing and fixed it to their door, perhaps,
they hoped to calm its humming, to bind it
to the order of their ordinary days, as you do now,
trying not to touch it with your fingers
as you pull it from the ground.

Field School

After the earthquake, you see
a biblical swarm of locusts. You're bitten
sixty-four times by gnats. The lukewarm Caribbean
smells of kerosene. A tropical storm is sleeping
in your bed in the hotel, tossing and turning
with tears, as heaven leaks
through the roof. It is difficult
to eat anything, for the air itself stinks of
the rotten scent of an unknown tree.
In the earth's trembling, the tunnels
beneath the hieroglyphic stairway cave in;
the statue of 18 Rabbit loses the glyph
of his name. When the group returns
from the beach, the plaza has been riddled
with bullets, blood splashes
the walls and sidewalks. A man
from La Entrada was targeted by four
"assassins," but, in this country, an assassin
is anyone who is given an AK-47
and a few lempira a day—and the "target"
escaped into the church. Four villagers
were killed as the gunmen sprayed his getaway.
Tonight in Copán Ruinas, someone else
is childless, motherless, fatherless.
It's not magic how things keep disappearing.
Each year it's harder to keep the jungle
back. In the towns, you see men, never
women. At times, you wonder if
the women are all that's left of the ancient Maya, hiding
in their houses without doors or windows,
just slashed-out openings that keep nothing out.
And the gods? They stream up by the thousands

out of the ground, devouring everything
within reach, a butterfly or two, an insect, several birds,
down that pathway where the children of the jaguar
are still playing ball with human heads.

The Discovery

The equatorial sun seems to have hands
pressing down upon anything that moves,

urging every body back into the shadows,
back into that offertory box buried

beneath the ancient altar of Copán. In a late age,
the postclassic villages were trying to revive

old gods with new sacrifices: Tlaloc and his "goggles,"
the newly flayed skin of a man loosely ringing his eyes,

the integumental shroud worn to renew the god's powers
to peer into the realm of the dead.

When nothing came of the sacrifices but more
sacrifices, Copán was abandoned, its doors ceremonially closed;

the Navel of the World was buried.
But now a new age is drunk with discovery.

And though the ants stream up out of the disturbed
crevices like the enraged children who survived the flood

that drowned the last world, though tonight
José will be beheaded with a machete,

though in the morning Pedro will be run over,
though it will rain in the hours when it never rains,

and an earthquake will collapse the sacred
tunnels, nothing will stop this relentless unearthing,

deeper and deeper into the earth, until the mind crosses
a threshold of salt and disturbs the baby snake:

its black body and red head, no less venomous
for being newly hatched.

Ceremonial Trash

Raptors, turkeys, psittacine, and
    quail at Chaco with their wings removed,
        "the dirty quail" of the Aztec constellation
        nibbling on the bones
            of the gods, sacrificed as the filthy bird
            of concupiscence.
Any bird that could strike or sing was holy,
according to the interred wings: at Pueblo Alto—
golden eagle, hawks, mountain bluebirds.
      Mammals were beheaded,
          birds were dewinged;
what shall we say of the meticulous
debeaking of macaws?
        The fully articulated
twelve headless turkeys, the dogs burned as witches?

There is no essential difference between
animal sacrifice and human sacrifice,

we know this from the lack of interments,
the excavations of *flocks of children, their*

wings used as fans.

Room of Dust

Acrid, the earth falls upon our hands,

it clings to our clothing;

it is silk, and when a hand

traces something in the depths of the floor,

we cannot read it: it is written in the lost language

that the feet of a drunken man scrawl upon the ground

as he staggers his way home one morning.

We vanish upon entering this room;

the earth inhales us... we enter the nostrils

of the rain. We go on anyway, we cannot stop.

We know we are walking

into a mouth, the mouth

of that cave where God sits,

a tired vagabond or exhausted tour guide at the entrance,

and waits at the threshold to gently push us in. One by one

we are devoured by beauty. We cannot stop

being born.

The Sacrifice Tree

Interrupting the horizon with the languid lightning
of its black-and-white flight, a magpie flew
toward us, squawked, and folded up so quickly,
it seemed to collapse into a juniper tree
some twenty feet away where, shifting restlessly
from foot to foot, it cocked its head at us,

all the while clucking and scolding,
a current of iridescence rippling across its breast.
As we drew closer, the dark rainbow
of its wings rose into the air,
coasted, then dropped, into another tree
another twenty feet away.

Again we approached, again
the restless chattering, the halfhearted fanning
into the air, the floating descent
into a tree a little farther on.
Each time we drew closer,
the bird would shift its head from side to side

as if trying to see us
in a shifting mirror. Its gutturals,
full of clicks and whistles,
as it turned the prism of its gaze,
began to seem a kind of speech, full
of the stubs and clumps of meaning.

I remembered that man who claimed
that if you split the tongue of a magpie or raven,
it could mimic human speech. He raised pigeons
and kept a raven as a pet. The raven

was chained to a stump, and as we fled
his enclosure, shadowy with the beating of wings,

the raven had cried out, at random,
in an almost human voice. As we rode on
another magpie appeared, then another.
Together, they all began quizzing us, swiveling
their heads and muttering, as if we could understand
or answer. Finally, so many enveloped us,

we seemed to become part of the flock.
When we pulled our horses to a halt,
the flock circled us, shrieking, their wings shying
the horses onward until we came to a cedar tree.
There, in its heart—a great horned owl,
its back against the trunk;

its pupils drunk on light
could not focus on the magpies
who stabbed at it then jumped back
as the owl snapped open and shut
the great hook of her beak. To us
it seemed a place of awe, that shape

caught in a net of bird and branch,
for we could see the tiny white down
of her throat, the cut crystal of her stare.
We had never come so close, yet it was hard to look
into that face, stunned as it was by sunlight, while the tree itself
seemed to tremble with the black-and-white furies.

It made me tremble to think that the magpies called us,
with their arterial coaxing, to be assassins
of the owl. We heard them calling us to murder or to wonder,
yet the truth is we never knew what they wanted.
In the branches of that tree, their voices
seemed like static, a random frequency

from which a clear melody would never arise.
We could only sense in the white noise the approach
of something like meaning, the muttering
of the primordial world itself, calling out to us,
trying to fix us forever in the bright
gaze of the vanishing birds.

Heart of the Sky

roots in the bitterness
of this ground, spreads out the web of its hair,

the fine galaxy of its rootlets, an inch deep in every direction,
to live upon infrequent rain.

It opens its armored buds
and is pollinated for only one night—

a riot of sweetness—tongued
by a female brood of migrating bats.

At noon, its perplexed shape nests in the skeletal core
of a perished giant.

It steers always in the same direction, toward
the emptiness at the center of heaven, as its tongue

keeps worrying or trying to heal
the tiny sore inside its mouth.

It mocks the sentiment of the feathered sign
tacked up along the road, as it flies past,

flying onward, always flying away to the underbelly
of the world. It is always opening

useless wings within us. It hopes
to envelop its children in some haze or halo, hopes

to survive the gaze of the sacrificial quetzal, the lacerating
beak of the macaw. It's just another herald

flagging in the terrible heat, running up and down
the dried riverbeds that once ran between

the heavens and the underworld, racing on the roads that still belong
to the Lords of Fever, Pus, Pestilence.

No matter how little it rains, how prolonged the drought,
even when it cannot afford leaves, it blossoms…

all those multiple yellows that hummingbird and bat are drawn to,
sinking their heads into the nectar, the unfailing sweetness of the heart.

The Blue Mustard

The pot with its smoldering black
and white that appears to be carrying
stars is the vessel that reminds
me of my daughter, for she, too, is
a star, brightly burning
in the distance, as she charts
the constellations moving
into and out of
the spirals of heaven.

My first visit, so many years ago to these ruins—
bent over, racing through the doorways
through which I had to fold myself
like a fetus wishing to be born—
gave me the feeling of entering
a room where the window
was not a window but a portal
to another world, made me settle here,
root in these four corners, this earth.

And now, revisiting the ruins,
wandering among the artifacts
extracted from so many other
vanished lives, I see among
the pots—the shape of a puffer fish
blown up by its own fear,
the dream of a fish in the desert,
a spout with the horns of a goat—
not only the shape of my own life

but my daughter's.
So many fronds, delicate

hair of the earth, tiny clusters
of stars on the innumerable stems,
have grown from the seed
of a single moment,
like the blue mustard
now blooming
along every path.

Daphne: or how the soul falls
in love with what it will become

There were doubtless many others planted
around the compound of conference buildings
for shade and decoration, each with a ring
of grass or brick to contain its
lithe desire.

Yet that morning rushing
to my car for the long drive home,
I was gripped by the ordinary
birch, its white trunk like an arm rising out
of the earth.

Each leaf, turning singly,
wheeled as one, silver undersides flashing
into a single limb of light. Awake,
I was completely awake with becoming
that tree.

Galileo in the Year 2000

I tell you, it was never the Earth
that ended, the round verdant
globe itself humming with mud
and lava, but what we called
"earth," meaning the ideal plane
of our own existence.

In that Realm, its four corners
delineated by the rising and setting
of the sun, the equinoctial
possession, we, as Socrates said
moments before his death, nestled
in one of the hollows

and remembered
only the deluge. The Great Flood
so haunted our dreams
that we kept trying to pack up
what we could rescue, vacating
our Real.

For we had forgotten the names
of the stars. Like those peasants,
our fathers, who hoped to dredge the depths
of heaven, we cast a line out, spooling out,
into the night sky, and drew up nothing but the skull
of a horse, its ancient, antiqued head.

But it was only the ancient bodies
of the gods wheeling
out of sight, and something new,
unbearably bright, beginning

its helical rising. Out in the desert,
a Navajo woman is struck by lightning.

She begins to glimpse the Rainbow Deities.
They visit her. They eat. In the sky
over the Hopi reservation
a comet approaches, trailing
its shimmering hair,
and among the places of Desolation

that we have created upon the earth
sprout the tiny seedlings
of unknown species. A deer
in Vietnam grows canine teeth
and begins to eat meat
and to bark like a dog.

We do not know what is
or is becoming. Once, we were planted here
by the stars. We were scattered
like seeds upon the ground. We are just beginning
to open. We are just
coming awake.

POÈTE
MAUDIT

A History of Romanticism

Byron, Shelley, and Keats, I said
their names like a sweet resuscitation, saving
me from the laundry room, the din
of the washers, as I carried
as many sheets as I could
to the maids waiting to shape
the billowing whiteness to a stranger's bed.

The powers of the dead were everywhere.
I had heard them whispering
in my lover's mouth. They were the crowd
at the edge of the fourth-story roof, promising
us wings. They dug a pit in the backyard
of the house my parents rented, and slowly filled
the rooms with the sewage of acrimony and loss.

Byron, Shelley, and Keats, almost sublime when chanted
into the twentieth cup of the dregs
of coffee, or while filling in the schedule books,
our lives counting down at $1.35 an hour,
while the men who called for maid service—*Maid
of Athens, milkmaids, dairymaids, housemaids, any sweet maid*—
answered the door, stark naked, displaying a *Playboy* magazine.

"Peacocks" we called
the insurance salesmen, the corporate VPs
who arrived every week, fanning
open their newspapers and wallets,
their cock-a-doodle-do of glittering
watches and polyester suits. *Lord
George Gordon Byron,*

I knew I knew nothing
of the powers of the dead, though I could hear the clank
forged to every ankle *reluctant in a fleshly*
chain and had glimpsed the angel of division,
Lord Percy Bysshe Shelley, separating
the look in every eye from what lived
behind it.

While the supervisor went through
the rooms like suspicion, I hummed
she walks in beauty like the night
with Mrs. Ham. At seventy, she couldn't
afford to retire, and when her head grazed
the bed she was making, she'd fall asleep
still standing on her feet.

And all that's best
of dark and light meets in her aspect
and her eyes, and I thought of thee,
Augusta, and thee, mad Ottoline,
when three Navajo sisters shared
one husband, and *how we'll go no more*
a-roving so late into the night,

when Ann, the desk clerk, was embarrassed
every morning as she exited a stranger's room,
her hair still tousled by desire and,
how I would meet thee with silence
and with tears, when Mary Lou, the desk clerk,
on the phone every morning as lonely as the abandoned
Harriet, drove her car into the river.

I had gone to work
to taste the iron bit in the jaw of the world,
but hadn't counted on this. At the end of the day,
among the stones I stood a stone, exhausted,
waiting for a ride home, and felt my life draining away
into a sea of stagnant idleness, and I remembered
that woman who said, "Oh no, I'm fine, sweetie, just fine,"

when I was sent by her husband
to check on her. I hadn't been able to see
into the darkened room because she had chained
the door, her voice so kind and muddy
because her blood was draining
into the tub, and *O God! it is a fearful thing
to see the human soul take wing.*

Sometimes walking across the parking lot,
I would hear the cry of the peacocks
on the other side of the concrete wall.
An eccentric widow
kept a flock in her barren orchard —
all that was left of a once thriving farm —
and their cries erupted at random

throughout the day, a sound
like something being pierced, or strangled,
a sound like the power of death
entering the larynx, though it was, in fact,
the ruthless desire to go on, to perpetuate
oneself at any cost that so
tore, *filling their bare and void interstices.*

Byron, Shelley, Keats, one day on coffee break,
I told a Navajo woman some of the stories
of their lives, and she shook her head
and said, "Boy, you sure have weird friends."
How could I answer her? *I saw their thousand years of snow*
and, in her laughter, heard what was mute and rising
out of the sheets and the stone.

Poète Maudit

1

His father kept two praying mantes, pets
in the kitchen, leashed with one chain, the eye
of a broken necklace clipped around
each neck. In tandem, they consumed all
the cockroaches and pale silverfish, until,
one morning, nothing was left but each other.
Father himself now, he still expects to find
at dawn, the chain, its empty finding.
Lost in the kingdom of earwigs, Night Watch,
he looms over the nest of his son, slathers
him with baby powder, changing a diaper,
la la la, imparting to that hapless
grin the night ditty of his own sadness:
Clack, Clack, exoskeleton, murder in the heart.

2

Her lover had taken her dog for a walk,
when her neighbor's two wolf-dogs bounded
over the hill, released from their radio-
controlled collars, as if the owner in so
doing unleashed something in himself.
Her pet, her sweetie, was already "scraps" —
three-legged, one eye like a crazed marble,
an ear, a shred of flag — and now her vocal
cords being pulled out, while her lover drove
useless fists deep into the wolves. What a strange,
persistent muse, the muse of aftermath.
Miraculously, the dog survives: oh what a rag,
her bark, now a kind of wheezing, a song
clenched between God's teeth.

Apocrypha

As in *of spurious authorship:* as in Joan
of Arc may have been a follower of Dianus,
the ancient Mother God.

As in *of spurious validity,* that is, the people
may have followed her, because to all the secret
followers of Dianus, Joan herself
was God incarnate, because the ancient Mother
could take the form and face of anything, even
a tree, an animal, or a woman.

As in *the book that must be burnt,*
originally said *of any writing,* because those voices,
mythic, fabulous, were not the voices of known angels, but the *fictitious*
utterances of the wildflowers of a fairy ring, the *counterfeit*
prophecies of the sacred oak.

As in *what must be cast out,* as she herself was cast out
for wearing a man's clothing, her limbs banished to ashes and smoke.

Hidden, secret, as how she began to live, after her death,
dispersed into every imagination, each mind an *apocryphy* for her ardent image,

as in *of doubtful authority,* as in our own time the pope
declared her to be a saint, as if he himself were a true *apocryphalist,*
trying to reclaim her for the crypt, *apocryphate God,*

as in *her heart was cast into the fire,* as in *what refused to burn.*

Babel

All I remember of graduate school
is Fred in the first workshop; he was drunk:
his flight, a course of miniature drinks,
and he sounded like the dazed believers
who, every Sunday at my local church,
believed they could speak in tongues. Yet
for an instant, he came awake, as my peers parsed
my poem, "St. Rose of Lima." The poem reminded
him, he said, of being a tourist in Italy,
in the chapel of an uncorrupted saint,
this lovely girl in a nun's garb, locked
in a glass case; she looked as if just fallen
asleep, but was three hundred years dead.
He was afraid to enter, for he was a good
Baptist boy, and the room was, in fact, a cemetery.
Then, out of nowhere, a voice: *"What language
do you speak?"* He looked around — nothing
but the saint lying there. Then the question
came again, *"What language do you speak?"*
Three times, he was called, like Samuel
awakened by the voice of God, and, as he spoke,
he transfixed us with his gaze, as if, as if…
When, at last, he crept into the room, dared
to approach the corpse, he saw in the corner,
behind a door, a wizen nun offering him a choice
of guidebooks or audiotapes in different languages.
He laughed and most laughed with him, relieved
to be released into anecdote, the Pentecostal
joke of authorship and origins, because
it was easier than hearing God, or the Universe,
for even an instant, turning upon us to ask:
What language do you speak?

Reproach

to those who thought to be my teachers

What bees make
of the flower is honey,
the hectagonal
comb,

but what the flower makes
of the bees is flower,
itself, the hectagonal
bloom.

The Lesson

Fuck you, fuck me, I could have said to all
my teachers. But I was meek as a caterpillar
falling out of a tree. It clung to the spool
of its own being, a raveling from its gut.
When I had mercy for my teachers,
they had none for me, they worked with me,
as a farmer works a field, all methodology
of tine or plow, paid tenants, or the man
working for himself who kicks a sleeping
calf to rouse it and knows that it's thoroughly
frozen only by its entrails spilling out.
But I was as useless as that worm, struggling
on the ladder of the self, trying to spin
its way back to leafy heaven.

Just then a teacher came by, the one who
touched my face with her hand and insisted
that she loved me, the one whose only lesson
was that I should stop writing, stop breathing;
who cared anyway? She paused as if weighing
the scene and, with an air of terrible calmness,
dismissed me, the caterpillar, all idea
of rescue with a shrug of the Fates.
In her soul, that ancient farmland where mercy
meant no more than putting out of its misery,
a snake with a broken back was forever
writhing out of view. What she missed
was the marvel. That useless caterpillar was God's
finger writing its way through empty air.

The Worst Form of Ambition

attached as a leech attaches itself to
the underside of a great animal
fording a stream, is not
ambition for oneself or for paltry
limousines or crowds, but ambition
for the beast one rides upon—
so rare an aardvark...
one's Work or Art.

The Dead Are Translated into Another World

I sleep in the basement of my dead
uncle, a prizewinning taxidermist, who hung
six mule deer, two elk, two pronghorn antelope
upon the wall. They are almost alive,
their liquid gazes watching the vacant
meadow of his den. As I fall asleep,
layers and layers of leaves bury me, light
as the weight of animal sadness. I am falling
in a wood where death is a forest beyond counting.
At morning's green shiver, a sliver of light
through the cracked wall, I wake up, from a dream
of my dead uncle. He is standing in a clearing,
and, though he is stuffed like the animals
that he taxidermized, he looks as he did
when he was young. Such a quiet
and gentle man, he would ask the farmers
for permission to collect the rare albino magpie roosting
in their yard and would use a BB gun and aim
for the bird's eye to damage the plumage
as little as possible. In his workroom,
a plastic deer is still waiting to be shrouded
in the hide of the dead deer it was meant to embody,
as my uncle's hands hang uselessly at his side.
Sad in the pouch of his preserved
self, he stands naked in his almost eternal skin, an Adam
of balsa wood and sawdust, glass eyes and formaldehyde —
a rack of antlers, the only thing still living,
green, growing out of his head.

"*Let us go then, you and I*"

Pausing in the midst
of work, as a runner might pause

to check her pulse, I scan
the health of the nation

in the nation's words, reading
this poet, then that one,

the flu of solipsism on the page, the fluttering
diagnosis of the vague, the fatigue syndrome

of the arcane, until I am in a coma, a patient,
convalescent in a hospital bed, suffering

a malady from which no one ever dies but from which
no one ever recovers,

so caught in the drone of the anesthetic
injected into her veins and the monotone of the TV that hangs

from the rain-stained ceiling,
and the whine of the worn-out containers,

the emptied detritus of words, that
only the noise, the sharp grinding

of jet brakes, the squeal of the
pneumatic lift, the weight

of the tons screeching
on their appointed rounds, Thursday morning,

outside my house, on the other side of the window,
jolts me awake. It's

the trash truck, thank God,
the blessed trash truck.

Xena™ *in Philadelphia:* Isaiah's House

to Eleanor

Following my daughters
down Sixth Street, in our nondescript
shoes and jackets, our rumpled hair,
you and I shuffle like peasants muttering against
the Lords of the City on our way to the condemned
house that Isaiah has made into a work of art,
using slivers and shards of broken glass
to delineate human figures—the size of giants—
on the concrete walls, their bodies, lines
of a more than momentary shining, pieced together
out of fragments of light, as if lightning
had come down to earth and rooted in the stones.
    We are walking
as slowly as those peasant women
who, walking in the Andes, spin
a fine skein of llama wool
into a knot of rainbow,
but we, as we walk, are unraveling
the knot that binds us here,
the invisible knot that can be sensed
around the neck of the homeless man
who rises menacingly from the park bench,
the knot of the maimed pigeon's foot—
the blue pigeon that hobbles like Ahab
after the crumbs scattered like tiny coins
from someone's lunch sack—the knot
of the obtuse word that locks
the mind's Babel.
    Our hair is wild—

split ends rising in a chaotic nimbus
like the torn threads of an ancient tapestry,
or like the filaments of a new web casting
into the air—as you speak of a depth where sea turtles rise up
from gardens of coral or the roof of that cave
cracked like the human heart by a genuine vision
of something like God.

                In a dim shop lit with posters
of skulls, apocalyptic glow-in-the-dark
T-shirts, end-of-the-century
basement bargains,
my younger daughter excavates
from a corner of rubble, a life-size
stand-up of Xena™, "the warrior princess,"
and carries it away

                    like the flag of another world,
like a sword dividing the cloak of the past,
like a sandal shaking off the dust of condemnation.
As we enter shops, strangers greet not us
but the blue-eyed stare beneath the plastic wrap.
Laboring in her small shop, among the sputtering
globes of the candles, a woman runs
toward us, exclaiming how her daughter
always watches the show, though she herself
somehow always misses half of it, then blushes,
blurting out that she likes any woman who can
"kick a man's butt." As we wait in line at a wine shop,
a woman passing by growls, *"Xena"*
to the face and the form momentarily
anchored beneath my arm.

Like those Tibetan monks who crossed
the Himalayas carrying nothing but
a painting of the other realm, believing
that the divinity in the painting
would save them from the perils of the journey,
            my daughters lead us into their future,
its blue and measured gaze, where all the myths
are rewritten in the scroll of an ironic
sidekick, and gods are revealed as the small-time
thugs you and I always believed they were,
and, at the end of our ramble, we lead
them to a house of rubble, *Isaiah's House*,
where the artist has rescued every manner of ruin
and embedded it in the walls:
                        Blood-red plates scribbled with words,
the terra-cotta head of a goat, the serpent's
living calendar, metal gods whirling
like weather vanes on the roof, the arms
of the *Venus de Milo*, the head of the Medusa,
the blue wheel of Nahuatl, the lost pigments
for the fresco of war, the rubble of the tablets etched by the finger
of God, the catfish leaping in the Realm of the Dead,
the bricks of the tower that could have pierced
heaven, the nails and splinters that pierced us
again and again, the miniature cathedral
of the lost Ark and she who vanished from it,
the voice of the whirlwind, the torn song
of the whale, the fragments of the burnt
Sappho, the pearl of great price, the dented pans
of ordinary suppers, the cup of the sacred feast,
the flowerpots of our mother's kitchens.

          Whatever is
abandoned, shattered, lost, is
recovered in the very structure of this house
with its blue thresholds, its walls bearing the message,
spelled out in glass, in shining shards:

ART IS THE CENTER OF THE REAL WORLD.

Muse

In later years, my daughter said to me
that when she was little and before
sister and brother, growing up in that trailer
that bordered the desert, she thought there was someone
else who lived with us, and it was only later that she knew
there was no one else, just the poetry, that other child that I was
                                    always singing to,
nursing in my arms, chanting, as I passed back and forth between
                                    those rooms.

The Price of Books

I bent my back
to carry through all the cities
of Spain, up the hotel steps —
where the loaves of bread
from the bakery were waiting
every morning in their hot, crisp crusts —
the dictionary of the Real Academia. As I carried it,
I heard it whistling the whips of the flagellants
scourging themselves into Easter,
words of orthodoxy cockleburring
the flesh of my back, thorned,
by hook or crook to be transplanted, syllables
exact as bullhead or bee sting. *Libros*
that are not *libres*, even though, sometimes,
they languish, jacketless, torn,
on bargain tables, beneath the flags
outside Georgetown University,
or in the damp basement
of Salt of the Earth. For thirty-nine cents —
the bounty a pair of magpie wings
brought in Wyoming in 1968 — the sacred
manuscript of every indigenous people is remaindered
in a cardboard box. For thirty-nine cents, I carried the Huarochirí
manuscript home, a walking Andes of words, weaving
the suspension bridges of its myths across the white ravine
that swallowed the black llama and the heavenly fox,
written by those who knew they were vanishing
into cities where they would stand on corners
as beggars and be mistaken for mutes.
Books stapled together like wings, books like
the three perfect red leaves in which a child finds
the spine of her natal hour. Books possessed

by the flies of heaven, by the song of a sarcophagus,
by the face of that man crumpled
over a grate, by the soft thumping
of a moth caught in a screen of light,
by a kiss caught in a net
of hair. Books of the bulldozed
orchard where one or two surviving stumps
put forth a leaf, a branch. A book, alive, that dreams
of a world in a park in Madrid, flowering
with carnival tents, food booths, Peruvian musicians,
a splash of bitters tossed into a glass, people wandering
back and forth among the leaves of nothing
but books.

The Artist of Willendorf

What if it's true that "Venus," and all her other sisters
littering the Indo-European earth, began

in describing her own form?... not
by posing in a Venetian mirror

or moaning in the detached eye
on the delivery wall—

no more than a split fork
in another's road,

the art students stubbing out
smoldering bits of charcoal

on the curve of her shoulder—her hip
translocated into pears

or mountains with each erasure
and stroke... What if

standing in the interior of some thicket,
her nakedness was the beginning

of some clearing of the mind?
What if the exaggerations of her figure

are not the result of another gaze, exaggerating
his lust or her distance, but the result

of herself in some narrow glade turning her head
to look down upon her own thighs,

cocking her head backward to glimpse her flanks,
looking down upon her belly, then transposing

what the self felt like from within,
the body glimpsed by intuition's other, darker, eye,

into a cave full of darkness, that moment of bathing
in her own vision: faceless,

downturned head, arms that disappear
beneath the breasts or cross over them, transposed

into earth itself...?
Then wouldn't we have been the connoisseurs

of blindness, all these ages, caught in the blinding
surface of mastery and mirror...

When she stepped
into that pool of light on the forest floor

and looked down upon herself,
dappled by the shadows of the leaves,

what she entered
was the thicket of her own seeing:

the body seen from within itself,
holiness in all its parts.

THE
GIFT

The Foundling

The only ghost I've ever seen
was that of a baby black bear, waiting

for me one night in the kitchen in Salmon, Idaho,
a small green tornado caught in the corner by the stove,

full of pale yellow lights like the tiny polished stones
that flash in the bed of the coldest mountain streams.

All winter, we lived in that rented house, while the landlord,
in the garage, practiced his butcher's art, skinning, gutting, disassembling

whatever the local hunters brought him—and I'd seen the cub
hanging outside my window. Flayed of its rich black skin,

reduced to the scaffold of its bones, its overlay of red muscle and white fat,
without claws or snout, pud or tail of bear, it hung in the glare

of the porch light like a human child. So when I went roaming
the silenced house so late at night and was met by that wild presence,

I spoke to it until it sighed and vanished into the peeling wall,
and left me, the only child still there, snared in the net of the world.

Angel Fire

That day on the mountain, the stones began to speak,
as Christ promised—when he rode into Jerusalem,
and the scribes rebuked the crowd for such
a riot of outcry and song—*and if I hushed*
them, even the stones would rise up
and sing. The guides told us impending lightning
made the stones chat and clatter, clacking
in that meadow, at 14,000 feet, the rocks
shifting restlessly, shivering against one
another, tapping one another into sound,
in the gathering embrace of an electrical
storm. *If our hair should rise into a sudden halo,*
we should fall to our knees upon the ground.
But lightning isn't born of the nimbus. The stones sing
because electricity is rising from the earth—fingers
of invisible light, unseen streamers, rising
out of everything that is. So Job called down
the whirlwind, and in Michelangelo's painting,
it's Adam, lactescent and supine,
who lifts his hand and summons God to earth.
So in the beginning, a pulse must have reached out
of the primordial ooze, out of the stumps
and stubs of chemical compounds, calling
down the spark from heaven—the bolt
that would transform their static ladders
into fluid DNA. The flare of desire, the jolt
of becoming always rises out of the earth.

A Dram of Bitters

"Bitters" are not bitter, are not
injurious, ancient instruments
of torture, cruel flavorings
of death, are not "the proper pain
of taste" (according to Bain, the baneful),
but a small bottle of bitters, a drop
or two, makes the orange juice brilliant
in a glass of gin and quiets
the stomach when it is unsettled
by true bitterness — whatever
in the world is "hard to swallow"
or admit, the crumb of cruelty
caught in one's craw, the iron bit
gnashing in one's teeth, the baleful
bile of "what has to be"
tasted to extremity.
Which is probably why
the British, intoxicated
in South America, copyrighted the recipe
into the colonial world
to try and make purgative,
a medicinal substance,
out of their own doubtful history,
caught between sour peevishness
and virulence of action
and of feeling — chugging the wild plenty
of the bitters down. But, no, bitters
is something more than "a noggin
of lightning, a quartern of gin." A secret
recipe distilled from the bark of the tree
of life, the original verb of an aboriginal sensibility, the surviving
noun of the cloud canopy in Venezuela, the genealogy

of a mindful tribe, the undiscovered draught
of mercy—not extract of gentian
or quinine or wormwood, those Old World
poetic distillations—but something vegetable,
persistent, extending roots into the world.
An autochthonic brew. Who tastes it,
tastes sweet earth.

On a Winter's Night

*At dawn, as Jesus was returning to the city,
he felt hungry. Seeing a fig tree by the
roadside he went over to it, but found nothing
there except leaves. He said to it, "Never
again shall you produce fruit!"; and it
withered up instantly.*

It's the cursed fig tree, backlit, a bitter
halo in the distant lights, though I don't know
how it came here, transplanted, still out
of season, surviving amputee of God's will.
The man who climbed into a fig tree to glimpse
Christ in the crowd was blessed, but the barren tree
was blasted, lopped-off by a word from Christ,
to forever signify all fruitless souls.
A trope of useless love, it grips now a clay hill
in this Southwestern desert, and what I see
is how it thrives, as love does, stubborn beyond
the pointing finger, beyond the uttered curse.
For while its limbs are but stubs, it's dense
with life, so many new sprouts sporting out
of its trunk and roots, it rises within the thicket
of its own persistent self.

Gordian Knot

In the groin of my infant son, twin hernias,
each the heft of a small stone, caught
in the fists of his abdomen, made him howl
in Toledo. We raced from the villa, down
the mountain toward the picturesque view,
through the gates named for the blood-red
color of their stones, down the darkened
streets, repeating to the policemen, *Mi hijo,*
mi hijo, está muy enfermo, muy enfermo,
and in the lobby, as we waited, they carried
out a little girl, naked, shrieking, some plastic
apparatus, like a strange clear diaper,
attached to her, and they carried her by
her arms, her limbs flailing, and dropped her
into her mother's lap, and when the doctors
finally spoke to us, I heard their Castilian
as if it were English, and as they removed
his diaper, I saw the knots of the hernias
had unraveled, the intestine withdrawn
out of view, and everything was as it should be,
back inside his body, and we drove back to the villa,
ceremonious and leisurely with good luck and Thank Gods,
and one of the two cranky, ancient brothers who ran the inn
was waiting for us outside the gate, beside the ancient
olive press, and as we told him what had happened,
we looked down toward the plain of Toledo, and
fireworks were exploding in the sky, a feast day
in a small village outside the gates, as if the universe
were welcoming us back, all that color breaking,
glory and mercy and mercy and unspeakable relief.

What We Need Words For

Each morning, his baby fingers clack
on the electronic keys of the obsolete typewriter
that my father left us when he died,
and what my son hears and loves is the sound
of his own fingers clattering into the world, the zing
of the carriage return, the space bar like a runaway train
clicking through the letters that he is only beginning
to recognize, the hunt and peck
of his own name.

We all stumble into ourselves
like this, fitting our fingers to the shape of letters,
while the page gallops out of our reach,
and, though he's only five, it's loss that drives him
to the words, trying to pick out his own name
among whatever is attached to himself, whatever
he longs to answer, relating each day
a letter to his sister, now gone from home,
far away in college.

The page, when it rolls off the cylinder,
is full of the rhythm of his furious
digits, all drive and urgency of expression,
a jumble of letters and numbers, not words,
not legible text, but a sea of drift,
and, yet, at times, in the broken lines,
a name, a word, floats up into view —
the first legibility of the heart, its exacting
infancy — *lluv   luve   yur broder   Jacob.*

The Inheritance

My daughter was born with a blue moon
at the base of her spine. "A Mongolian spot":
Hopi children on Third Mesa are born with it,
as are the great-great-great-grandchildren of the Huns
who fled defeat in Rome to settle quietly
in the cantons of Switzerland... Unclaimed
fathers and mothers claim us in the flesh
of our children; the birthmark grips us by the heels.
When my son was running a fever, I discovered
the distorted shapes of Africa, South America,
floating on his tongue, I worried it was something
terrible, strep throat gone horribly wrong.
The doctor laughed and said it was nothing,
just a case of "geographical tongue." All his life,
he would bear this map of lost Pangaea—its continents
now altering and flaring to a baby's health and mood.

Internal Clock

In the morning, their heads vised
between the pillows, my daughters try to hush the world:

the bright peep at the window, the grinding
of the espresso machine, the cacophony of piping.

At night, so late the moon is falling
back into the sea, they're improvising

a rap song, with click and cluck
of mouth and tongue, to keep the world awake.

I tell myself they're just teenagers—and, thank God,
not like those streaming in an erotic medley of stoned

cars through the Safeway parking lot every night—that this
is why they mimic bears caught in unpredictable seasons.

But the fact is I'm the one who's growling, ranging
through their rooms, as if rummaging for what I've lost,

and they're just children craving what I cannot give—
eye of lover, hand of friend—and the love

that I still can. So they go on trying to block out
my morning racket,

and I to tone down their twosome at two AM.
Still, for all the awkwardness of this mooring, the stem

of something labors, creaks, joyfully breaks free,
as they move into a time beyond me,

and, at moments, we find ourselves in some noon
or midnight, laughing, cutting up, unable to stop urging one another

into inconvenient song.

Voice of the Sphinx

"It's not true that, in despair, I threw myself
into the sea or became that bronze curiosity
of the Middle Ages—male, guarding
a secret larder. To escape those
who kept hunting me, I transformed myself
into a small brown sparrow, nondescript.
That crowd with spears and nets
pursuing me through the whitewashed villages
never guessed that what they so feared—a sacred monster,
a woman, with the claws of a lion, wings of a bird—
could take on the shape of the ordinary,
could hide in the hollow of a river
where the grass throngs with goslings every spring.
There are so many sparrows in the world
they would never notice one more,
trembling at the edge of a swamp, hidden in the depths
of the branches. So for thousands of years
I have been sitting here, clutching this perch, thinking
and thinking my way back, dreaming my way
into the dreams of your daughters who already feel
rude wings beginning to prickle, erupting
from their shoulders, at the moment they awake."

Headlock

I was the caped bat, wings flaring from my shoulders,
whom the others followed down the hill, a girl
leading all the boys in thundering
descent, so he had to make a point
of beating me, on that cold day,
when the drifts and whistles of the snow
creeping in the doors kept us inside
playing marbles, where I won for keeps
his tawny-eyed shooter, his favorite steelie,
and all his blue-eyed cats. All of a sudden,
he grabbed me, using his only lethal move,
and I was on my hands and knees, like a dog
on its belly, grabbed by the scruff of the neck.
Yet he was not strong enough to hurt me,
so we froze in a tableau of display
and shame before the other second-graders.
I knew that I could grab him by the head and flip
him over my shoulder onto the cold tiles
and knew, too, it would seriously hurt him.
I was strong enough to do it, at seven
had already pummeled the bullies who locked
my three-year-old sister out of the house;
had stood in the chicken yard at the age of five,
and, waiting for the bus, bloodied the face
of the eight-year-old who meant to teach me
a lesson. But I paused that morning, for whatever
reason, thinking my way through the fog of embarrassment
into the deeper fog of anger, where something cleared
into a brightness, a clearing within me, a kind of meadow—
ground to stand on, air to breathe, and mercy in the world.
I let him go, he let me go, we let each other live.

The Gift

I was wrong when I compared the mask of my own face
to an artifact, some kind of relic, or the shed skin of a snake.
That day, there was no wounding. At the museum,
that morning, when the woman was teaching
the children how to make masks of their own faces
with the plaster-of-paris bandages that doctors use
for instant casts, I was glad to lather
my daughters' faces with lotion, to place the wet strips
on their faces, and later to feel on my own face,
the patting of their hands like the beating of eyelashes against
my cheeks. The fine grit of dissolved earth floating
on my skin was pleasant, cool, and, afterward, choosing
the colors to paint the mask was like selecting one's own
plumage: Ann's singular purple, Maria's
black and white splashed with orange, my turquoise.
When I was holding the shape of my own face in my hand,
it was nothing like a death mask. I saw how easy it was
to put the self aside and pick it up again. It wasn't the sacrificial mask
I'd seen in Mexico—a human skull inlaid with lapis lazuli, a
                                    merciless reduction—
but a moment of happiness, a fragile shell, the gift
of mother and daughters, when, laughing,
we shaped one another into being
by touching what we were.

Caught in the Nets of Illumination

Lord, my lyghtnyng, flashes over the rims of Utah
where we are hemmed by pitchforks of light
and driving through a rain that evaporates
before it can touch the earth. A spire pierces
the flank of a hill, and fire leaps forth from a real
burning bush, clearly visible, twenty miles away. They say
where lightning touches is hotter than the sun. No lucid
veil, this storm, but a fist of the Father *whiche sendeth lyghtelyng*
to the destruction of myscheuous men — heaven's
arrhythmia jarring one's own electrical pulse. My father,
as a young man, was riven by lightning, arrested
as he stood by a chain-link fence. No *spiritus paraclitus*
that in the *lyknesse of a lightnynge* lit upon the world,
the strike imparted no grace or wisdom, was as meaningless
and incomprehensible as the jabs of his invalid father.
He woke up later, lightning pains around his heart,
rain misting on his face, and said nothing of God's blow,
except by implication when he spoke of his training as a boxer
that *no human being* could knock him out.
Years later, lightning came into our house, forked
through an upstairs window, and shed light upon the vanity
where my sister's reflection was putting on her makeup;
and, as children fishing in a mountain meadow,
we all fled a net of lightning. Like the tiny brook trout
we had been catching in the small cold
branches of the stream, we leapt and trembled
at hook and gaff. We ran and ran
from the Almighty shrouded in thunder
on that mountain — vertical, always discharging
from above to below, every wing
nesting in heaven meant to raptor us
with a crushing blow. Our mischievous laughter

silenced by this storm: my six-year-old son fears
the encircling hedge of God, the bright scowl of the nagging elders,
and keeps asking what happens if… if lightning strikes our car,
and he's calmed only when his father says, "Don't worry,
lightning rarely strikes a car. The rubber wheels
are insulated from the earth, and all that lightning
really wants is to get back to the earth."

Autochthonic Song

We knew the buffalo were dangerous, but, most of the time
as we drifted among them, longing to touch

the bright curls of one of the spring calves,
their coats the color of new pennies, they lowered

their heads to the wild grasses, and shied away
only when we drew too near. For months

we moved among them, circling
the sweet expressions of the calves,

as they kept circling that hill that seemed a ziggurat,
pointed at the summit, like that odd vision

of Columbus—off the coast of South America
"the earth was round and something rising

in the distance like a breast"—who thought
he had reached the beginning

of all creation, the nipple
of time and space. The hill glittered

with mica—flakes, the size and breadth
of a human hand—scattered

over its flanks. We tried many times to bevel by hand
the stones into a clear plane, an eyeglass

through which we could view the world,
but the crystals only split along the cleavage,

until, running among that shaggy tribe,
we forgot our mothers, our fathers, as if, running among

that remnant, we could save some part of ourselves
from extinction. Crazy with liberty,

I veered toward a calf, drew so close
that I could never remember

if I had touched it or not. But the mother,
her malevolence, one movement with her desire

to protect, wheeled in alarm,
and as she did so the herd wheeled with her, as a flock of sparrows

will turn in the sky to enfold a red-tailed hawk. A current
of rippling fear or anger, the buffalo

turned to charge us. We ran, the breath scattering
out of our child-lungs, barely able to keep ahead

of that rhythm that had always seemed like that of a choppy
rocking horse but which now seemed as fluid

as a flash flood churning down an arroyo.
We ran toward the hill, hoping the slope would save us

by wearing them down, the climb exhaust their fury,
and it did, but so slowly that by the time the buffalo stopped,

milling about halfway up, we were ourselves stampeding,
seized by a panic, so ancient, it kept our ribs

splintering in our chests all the way up the hill
until we crammed ourselves into the tiny cave

at its summit, clinging to ourselves
among the black widow spiders, the sloppy cobwebs

of fear, and it was only then that I understood—
the earth is not our mother but a wild music beyond the self.

Notes

Many of the "quotes" in this book are invented, and those that are borrowed are usually borrowed from memory, not copied from books, or, in some cases, are paraphrased from memory. In any case, I am responsible for their errors. In some of the poems, where a line was too long to fit the page, the remainder has been set flush right below it.

PROVISO

The quote "Faith (as you say)..." is from Shakespeare's *The Tempest*.

COMPARATIVE RELIGION

The phrases "gat no warmth" and "knew her not" are from 1 Kings, King James Version.

PARABLE OF SNAKES AND STONES

"Who among you if your child asked for a fish would give him a snake?" was said by Christ.

SAINT JOHN OF THE CROSS

"Even bound by the thinnest of golden threads, the soul's inexplicably bound" is from Saint John of the Cross.

"A LONELY MAN IN HIS GREATNESS"

I'm indebted for the title and the phrases "smelled of the absence of all scents," "no human presence should mar his daily stroll in the gardens," and "pure white wraith," as well as some of the facts, to *Hitler's Pope: The Secret History of Pius XII*, by John Cornwell.

THE RELIC

There's a story that a peasant spotted Saint Teresa of Avila in the river, where her mule had dumped her while crossing, and that she was shaking her fist at the sky and yelling, "The reason you have so few friends is that you treat them so badly." The story may be apocryphal, but she was to express the same idea in her writing, as she was also to say that she entered the convent because "it was better to suffer a lifetime as a nun than an eternity in purgatory." She was also to criticize those who were afraid of the devil or desirous of miracles.

FACE OF THE LEVIATHAN

The quotes "animalcules," "minute, despised creatures" and "endowed with as great perfection in its kind as any large animal" are from Anton van Leeuwenhoek, the inventor of the microscope.

GALILEO WAS FINALLY BURIED IN THE BODY OF THE CHURCH

"This is the finger... which scanned the heavens and spanned their immense space" and "That wondrous instrument which pointed to new stars..." are translations of the Latin verse of Thomas Perellius that is inscribed on the base that displays Galileo's finger.

EVERY CONSECRATED HEAD

"Every hair on your head has been counted, so do not be afraid" and "who can destroy both body and soul" are from the parables of Christ. "The lovely, the lively locked" is from Eleanor Wilner's description of the Medusa.

BETWEEN THE IMAGINED AND THE REAL

I am indebted to Stanley Moss for the "story" that ends the poem.

MY MOTHER'S HIP

2. "Suffering came into the world" is the translation for the name, Linus, of the unfortunate son of Psamathe and Apollo.

4. "The left hand knoweth not…" is from Christ's parables in the King James Version.

The Sacrifice Tree

Throughout this section, I am indebted to Ann Seiferle-Valencia for her conversations, rich with stories and insights and anthropological knowledge.

CEREMONIAL TRASH

"There is no essential difference between animal sacrifice and human sacrifice" is a quote from René Girard.

ROOM OF DUST

The idea of God sitting at the entrance of a cave waiting to push us in to be devoured by the beauty of the world is from Simone Weil.

A HISTORY OF ROMANTICISM

Most of the phrases are from Byron, though "reluctant in a fleshly chain," is, I think, from Shelley and "filling their bare and void interstices" is from Keats.

POÈTE MAUDIT

The title of the poem and the section are deliberately incorrect in French. I've used the feminine noun and the masculine adjective; "cursed poet" is meant to apply to and confound both genders.

REPROACH

There is no *hectagonal*. I made it up from the Greek *hect* or *hecto*, usually used to suggest a factor of one hundred. I intend for the amount to be unidentifiable.

XENA™ IN PHILADELPHIA: *Isaiah's House*

The artist, Isaiah, has written "ART IS THE CENTER OF THE REAL WORLD" with shards of glass or tile pressed into the walls of his house in Philadelphia.

ANGEL FIRE

"And if I hushed them, even the stones would rise up and sing" is Christ's rebuke to the Pharisees when they complained of the noise that the crowd was making as He entered Jerusalem.

VOICE OF THE SPHINX

I am indebted to Ann Seiferle-Valencia for this account.

CAUGHT IN THE NETS OF ILLUMINATION

"Lord, my lyghtnyng," "whiche sendeth lyghtelyng to the destruction of myscheuous men," and "lyknesse of a lightnynge" are from the *OED* definition for "lightning."

About the Author

Rebecca Seiferle is the author of two previous books of poetry, *The Music We Dance To* and *The Ripped-Out Seam*, and a translation of César Vallejo's *Trilce* (all from the Sheep Meadow Press). Her work appears in a number of anthologies, including *The Extraordinary Tide: New Poetry by American Women* (Columbia), *Best American Poetry 2000* (Simon & Schuster), *Saludos: Poemas de Nuevo Mexico, Poems of New Mexico* (Pennywhistle), and *New Mexico Poetry Renaissance* (Red Crane). Her work has won the Bogin Memorial Award (1991) and the Cecil Hemley Memorial Award (1998) from the Poetry Society of America, the Writers' Exchange Award from *Poets & Writers* (1990), and The National Writers Union Prize (1986). *The Ripped-Out Seam* was a finalist for the Paterson Poetry Prize, and her translation of *Trilce* was the only finalist for the 1992 PEN West Translation Award. She is the founding editor of *The Drunken Boat*, an on-line magazine of international poetry and translation. She currently resides with her family in Farmington, New Mexico.

ACKNOWLEDGMENTS

"'Animal People'" and "A History of Romanticism" appeared in *Alaska Quarterly Review*.

"The Making of Saints" and "'A lonely man in his greatness'" appeared in *Archipelago*.

"Comparative Religion" and "The Foundling" appeared in *Boulevard*.

"Voice in the Whirlwind" appeared in *LA Poetry Festival: Spotlight on Santa Fe*.

"Signs and Wonders" (under the title "Miraculum") and "The Dead Are Translated into Another World" appeared in *The Nebraska Review*.

"Toledo" appeared in *Partisan Review*.

"Law of Inertia," "The Argument," and "Modus Operandi" appeared in *Pif*.

"The Relic" appeared in *Ploughshares*.

"The Housewarming Gift" appeared in *The Poetry Porch*.

"The City of Brotherly Love Is Neither," "Poète Maudit," and "The Artist of Willendorf" appeared in *Prairie Schooner*.

The section entitled "The Sacrifice Tree" appeared as a chapbook of the same title in *Santa Fe Poetry Broadside*.

"The Face in the Depths of the Desert" and "Muse" appeared in *Snowapple: Wilderness*.

"Saint John of the Cross," "The Writing on the Wall," "The Lesson," and "Gordian Knot" appeared in *The Southern Review*.

"What We Need Words For" appeared in *The Sun*.

"If the Shroud of Turin Is a Fake" (under the title "Tin Cross, With Instruments of the Passion") appeared in *The Taos Review*.

"The Custom" appeared in *Wise Women's Web*.

The Chinese character for poetry is made up of two parts: "word" and "temple." It also serves as pressmark for Copper Canyon Press.

Founded in 1972, Copper Canyon Press remains dedicated to publishing poetry exclusively, from Nobel laureates to new and emerging authors. The Press thrives with the generous patronage of readers, writers, booksellers, librarians, teachers, students, and funders — everyone who shares the conviction that poetry invigorates the language and sharpens our appreciation of the world.

PUBLISHER'S CIRCLE

Allen Foundation for the Arts
Lannan Foundation
Lila Wallace–Reader's Digest Fund
National Endowment for the Arts

EDITOR'S CIRCLE

Breneman Jaech Foundation
Port Townsend Paper Company
Washington State Arts Commission

For information and catalogs:

COPPER CANYON PRESS
Post Office Box 271
Port Townsend, Washington 98368
360/385-4925
poetry@coppercanyonpress.org
www.coppercanyonpress.org

The typefaces used in this book come to us from the
Dutch Baroque. Janson Text is derived from the designs
of Hungarian traveling scholar Miklós Kis while he
worked in Anton Janson's Amsterdam workshop in the
1680s. The titles are set in Berthold Van Dijck Titling,
based on the work of Christoffel van Dijck,
from the 1660s.

Book design and composition
by Valerie Brewster, Scribe Typography.
Printed on archival-quality Glatfelter Author's Text
at McNaughton & Gunn, Inc.